CREATIVE
Frame-weaving

CREATIVE
Frame-weaving

CLAUDINE LOUW

Cape Town

Delos, 40 Heerengracht, Cape Town

Translated by Thea Brink
Photography by Siegfried Behm
Illustrations by Erna Schoeman
Cover design by Abie and Jasmine Fakier
Set in 11 on 13 pt Optima Medium and
printed and bound by National Book Printers, Goodwood,
Cape

First edition 1990

ISBN 1-86826-066-6

Contents

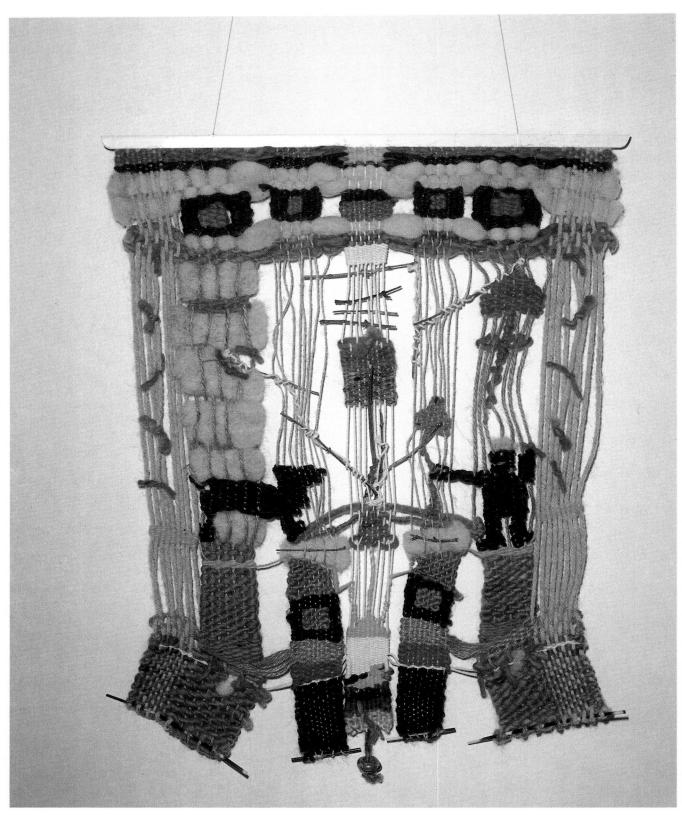

Photo 1
Experimental weaving with ethnic theme by Karen Koorts

Introduction

WHAT IS WEAVING?

Weaving is a method of interlacing two sets of threads to form fabric or cloth. These two sets of threads are called the warp and the weft. **See illustrations 1(a) and (b).**

The desire to create is inherent in man's nature, and this is especially true in the highly technological world of today, where goods are usually bought ready-made. Weaving is an excellent way of expressing one's in-born creative urge. Handweaving means different things to different people. It is a craft for making useful household articles, an art form for the artist, a technique for the therapist and a tool for the educator. Ultimately, it is also a means of reaching back to the origins of man.

THE ORIGINS OF WEAVING

From the earliest beginnings, weaving has formed an integral part of man's existence. It is one of the oldest and noblest of all occupations, originating in the Stone Age. Every weaver therefore forms part of a modern link in the very long chain of the history of weaving.

When one sees the weaver bird weaving its nest, one realises that the true origins of weaving are to be found in nature.

The first materials used for weaving were plant materials such as willow slats, reeds, bark, grasses, sugar cane, bamboo and palms. These woven or plaited articles were purely functional. **See illustration 2.** Later other materials such as animal hide, hair and wool were

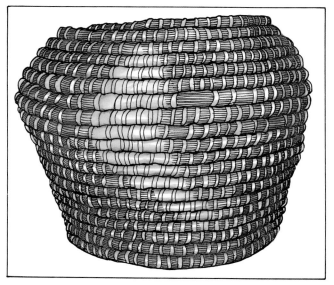

Illustration 2
The technique for weaving this basket has been used since the Stone Age, and is still in use in some parts of the world

used. While man was still a nomad there was little progress in weaving techniques, but when he began to settle permanently in one place, the upright weaving loom was soon developed.

One of the earliest methods of keeping a set of threads under tension for weaving was to hang them from a horizontal branch and weigh them down with stones. **See illustration 3.** The weaver stood in front of the threads and began weaving at the top, until he had to sit down to continue. The people of Lapland still use a similar method today.

In various parts of the world different cultures designed their own methods to stretch warp threads taut so that other threads could be interwoven. Through the ages the primitive weaving-frame evolved to a more stable version on which the desired results could be obtained more quickly and easily. Weaving looms and techniques still tend to differ from place to place rather than from age to age.

In various parts of the world the kind of weaving developed by a specific culture was influenced by the climate, the indigenous raw materials and the needs of the community. In Central Africa, for example, weaving was used to make articles for daily use and for protection against the elements. **See illustration 4.**

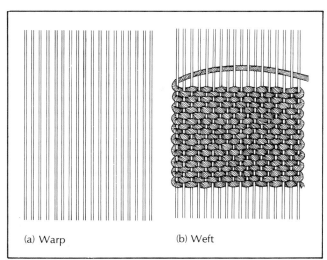

(a) Warp   (b) Weft

Illustration 1

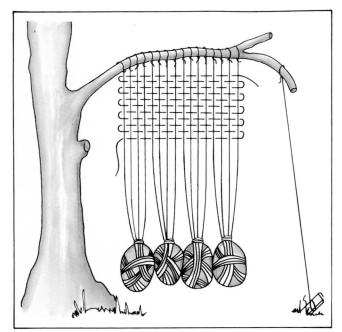

Illustration 3
One of the earliest kinds of frame looms. The branch and the stones at the bottom maintain an even tension so that the weft threads can be woven through

Five thousand years ago the Egyptians in North Africa were able to weave fine cotton and linen fabrics, and India and China were known since early times for the silk that was woven there. Later some parts of Europe also became renowned for their gold and silk fabrics, while England was widely acclaimed for its finely woven woollens and later also for its silks and cottons.

During the eighteenth century the growing demand for textiles and the demand for faster production methods led to inventions that resulted in the Industrial Revolution.

Illustration 4
Some tribes in Africa used the articles they wove from plant materials for shelter and for demarcation of property

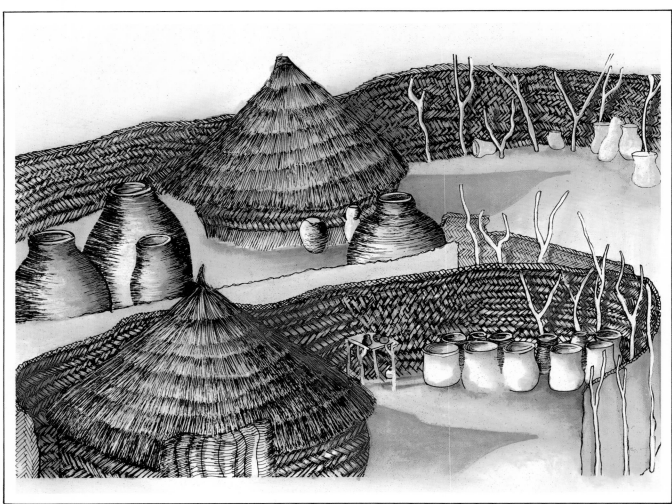

During and after this revolution the art of handweaving and its allied crafts nearly died out, except in some rural areas where it was preserved in the writings and records of master weavers. Fortunately it is possible to draw a very complete picture of the tradition of handweaving from these records.

When immigrants from Europe settled in the New World, there was again a need for simply woven fabrics for clothing and other household articles.

Research and new inventions continue to play an important role in the development of weaving. Some of the new equipment is highly complicated and intricate, and yet the basic weaving technique has not changed throughout the ages, whether one works on a simple hand-frame or a modern high-speed loom.

WHY CREATIVE FRAME-WEAVING?
Creative frame-weaving is merely one part of the whole spectrum of weaving. This book concentrates on this aspect as it is one of the most natural and economical ways of weaving. Creative frame-weaving is, in fact, increasing in popularity at present.

It is also a very adaptable form of weaving. Simple household articles such as cushions, runners, handbags and purses can be woven in coarse or fine textures, and it is moreover especially suitable for weaving wall-hangings and floor cushions. Creative frame-weaving is approached in an informal manner, as a means of self-expression for the creative person. The creative weaving process is a process of development and growth. When each new technique is mastered, horizons are broadened, and new ideas and possibilities are discovered with every piece of weaving.

Photo 2
A large variety of weaving threads. They include wool, mohair, hessian strips, leather strips, natural raffia, reeds and drift-wood

CHAPTER 1

Materials and equipment

MATERIALS

Threads are the raw materials with which a weaver creates. The texture and the ultimate use of the threads determine the visual and emotional impact of every woven article.

Threads are used for weaving, but they are often also the source of inspiration as well as much frustration. In order to avoid the latter, you should get to know the wide variety of threads available, and determine your personal preferences. **See photo 2.** You will get the feel of the textures of the various threads by touching them and learn by experience the appropriate use of each one.

When in doubt as to whether a specific thread can be used as warp or weft, simply weave a small sample to discover the effect of the thread.

The first step in the process of weaving is choosing the correct threads for warp and weft.

WARP
The warp is a set of vertical parallel threads kept under tension. They form the basis of all weaving. **See illustration 1(a).**

A fairly strong thread should be used as it will be kept under tension for a long time. Warp threads also have to endure much handling. The thread should not stretch and should be a little thinner than the weft.

For wall-hangings and rugs a four-ply linen thread is recommended as it fulfils all these requirements. Otherwise a strong cotton or woollen yarn may be used if it is twisted firmly and does not stretch. Ordinary cotton string used for tying parcels can also be used for the warp in wall-hangings.

Runners and cushions are usually softer than wall-hangings, and for these a cotton thread is recommended. Cotton is strong but not as stiff as linen. 100% cotton thread used for crocheting can also be used as a strong warp for fine or soft articles.

The beginner should avoid synthetic threads at first, as they are inclined to stretch.

WEFT
The weft is a separate thread which is passed over and under, and sometimes around, the warp. **See illustration 1(b).**

Almost all kinds of thread – wool, mohair, linen, cotton, silk or synthetic – can be used as weft. These threads can be of any thickness or texture, as long as they are thicker than the warp. When the weft thread is thinner than the warp thread, one can weave with two or more strands. New textures or colours are created by combining two or more threads, or by untwisting yarns and twisting them in new combinations.

Strips of material can also be used for the weft. Cotton, linen or raw silk (old or new) are cut into long strips about 1 cm wide.

Hessian should be cut into strips 2 cm in width as it frays easily.

Leather can be used as weft if it is very soft and cut into very narrow strips.

Remnants of loosely woven fabric such as upholstery and curtain fabrics can be unravelled and the threads used for weaving.

Raffia, cord, lace and satin ribbon are used for special effects.

Raw wool, mohair, cotton or silk provide interesting textures.

Reeds, laths, driftwood, bamboo and seed provide variety. Make sure that it fits into the theme of the work. As the warp cannot stretch and bamboo cannot bend, this kind of material is attached on top of the weaving by means of knots. **See illustration 49(b) of project 9.**

The choice of a particular weft is determined by the kind of article that one wants to produce.

For wall-hangings and rugs a fairly stiff kind of weft such as karakul rug wool is used, while a softer weft such as handspun knitting wool is more suitable for cushions and runners.

There is a wide variety of materials and threads from which to choose, and in the beginning you should exercise caution against using too many different kinds of thread in one work.

EQUIPMENT FOR FRAME-WEAVING

An added advantage of frame-weaving is the fact that the necessary equipment is easy and inexpensive to make. You can therefore easily acquire various frames of different sizes which will enable you to try out different techniques, textures and knots on one frame and then use them on another frame as part of a project. Provided the frame is not too big, it is an easily handled piece of equipment.

If you cannot make the frame, a sturdy old picture

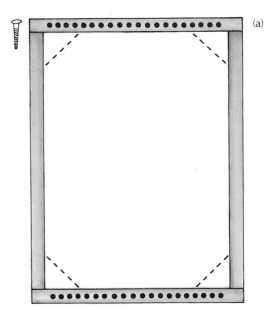

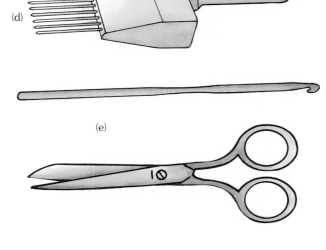

(a) A sturdy wooden frame with nails 1 cm apart

(b) A flat shed stick

(c) (i) A stick shuttle made of wood around which the weft thread is twisted

(c) (ii) Metal or wooden needle with which the weft thread is woven

(d) A wooden beater, with which to beat the weaving down

(e) Scissors and crochet hook

Illustration 5

frame or even a drawer is also suitable. Just make sure that the nails are inserted according to the instructions given below. Other equipment need not be specially made or bought either. A wooden ruler or flat piece of wood can be used as a shed stick, an ordinary kitchen fork as a beater and a butterfly used instead of a shuttle.

FRAME

The loom or frame is the piece of equipment that holds the warp threads parallel and under tension to form a shed through which to pass the weft. This definition holds true whether you use a simple nail frame consisting of four pieces of wood or a big complicated weaving loom. Each kind has its advantages and disadvantages.

The simple nail frame is especially well suited for crea-

tive weaving, and is the only kind described in this book.

Specifications for making two sizes are given. Projects 1, 2, 3, 4, 5, and 9 are woven on frame 1 and the others on frame 2.

	FRAME I	FRAME II
SIZE	50 × 76 cm	60 × 66 cm
REQUIREMENTS		
2 × crossbars	500 × 32 × 32 mm	600 × 32 × 32 mm
2 × uprights	700 × 32 × 32 mm	600 × 32 × 32 mm
Use hard wood which does not bend easily.		
40 mm nails (wire-nails)	2 × 43	2 × 51

12

4 × 50 mm
screws
sandpaper
cold glue

METHOD

Attach the crossbars to the uprights with cold glue and the screws, forming a rectangle. Drill holes in the cross-bars, 10 mm apart and in a straight line. The first hole should be 10 mm from the left inner corner and the last one 10 mm from the right inner corner. The diameter of each hole should be somewhat smaller than the diam-eter of the nails. Each hole should be 15 mm deep. Sand-paper the frame at this stage to prevent the threads from catching on rough edges. Hammer the nails in the holes, so that only about 15 mm of the nail protrudes.

If one drives the nails into the wood without drilling the holes, the crossbar will split.

A sealer may be applied to the frame.

Remember that the frame may be of any size, as long as it is sturdy and easy to handle. A frame may be bigger or smaller than the size given above. When the cross-bars are longer than one metre, it is necessary to add supports in the inner corner of the frame. **See illus-tration 5(a).**

The frame may be made to rest against a wall while you weave, or it may be held on your lap with the top of the frame against a table. You should try to find a com-fortable position as this kind of weaving is a slow process.

SHED STICK

The shed stick is passed over and under alternate warp threads to form an opening between them through which the weft threads may be passed.

The shed stick can be made from a piece of wood slightly longer than the width of the frame, about 38 mm wide and 8 mm thick. Sandpaper this piece of wood until it is smooth and the corners rounded off. If one end is flattened and rounded, the stick will be easier to insert. **See illustration 5(b).**

An ordinary wooden ruler can also be used, provided it is long enough to rest on the side of the frame.

STICK SHUTTLE
AND/OR NEEDLE

The shuttle or needle is used to weave the weft threads through the warp threads. Metal needles, 20 cm long, are very useful, and to be found at most knitting shops. A shuttle or needle can also be made from wood, about 20 cm in length. **See illustration 5(c)(i) and (ii).** The shut-tle and needle must be sandpapered until very smooth to prevent them from catching on the warp threads.

BEATER

A beater is used to push the weft thread down against the previous row. **See illustration 5(d).** A sturdy comb or kitchen fork can also be used.

OTHER EQUIPMENT

Ordinary tapestry needles, darning needles with sharp points, and a crochet hook are sometimes needed for finishing off the article.

A pair of scissors and a measuring tape are always used.

The design may be drawn on the warp threads with a permanent fibre tipped pen. Any other kind of ink will stain the weft threads.

CHAPTER 2

Techniques used in frame-weaving

Weaving ought to be a pleasurable process, enabling the weaver to express her ideas freely. This becomes possible when one has a thorough knowledge of the basic frame-weaving techniques and knots.

There are many techniques that may be applied and developed in frame-weaving, and the possibilities for creating striking and original articles are almost endless. The threads that can be used as warp and weft are available in many different sizes, colours and textures. The distance between warp threads may be changed. Either the warp or the weft threads, or both, can be visible. Weft threads can be woven, twisted or knotted into the warp threads in different ways. By combining different methods, different effects can be achieved. A few of these possibilities are described below.

The techniques and knots described in this chapter are definitely not all that can be said on the subject. Weavers all develop their own methods of weaving and tying knots. One method is not necessarily the correct one and the other the wrong one. If the method of weaving or tying knots results in a weakening of the structure of the weaving, it is obviously not to be recommended.

When using a specific technique, it is important to understand the reason or purpose of the technique and to be open to new ideas so that one can develop the most effective weaving techniques for the purpose.

It is easy to weave and just as easy to unravel. If the weaver wants to apply the technique in a new way or if she is not sure whether an idea can be executed, she should simply try it out. If the experiment is not successful, it can always be unravelled. The weaver will have gained in knowledge and experience.

The basic frame-weaving techniques and knots given below should first be practised and mastered before a project is attempted or else the weaving may easily deteriorate into a fight with threads.

THREADING THE WARP
Before the warp is threaded the correct type of warp thread must be chosen and the width of the finished article decided upon. On a frame with 50 nails on each crossbar, you can weave an article with a maximum width of 49 cm. On the same frame you can, however, weave narrower articles. For instance, if the width of the article should be 30 cm, you thread the warp over 31 nails.

The warp thread is tied around the top left nail. An ordinary double knot is sufficient. The head of the nail prevents the thread from slipping off. Then the warp thread is taken to the bottom of the frame, around the first nail on the left and back to the second nail at the top. **See illustration 6.**

The thread should always be tightened when it is wound around the nail. Try to keep an even tension throughout. The warp is threaded over the required number of nails and tied to the last nail with a double knot.

INSERTING THE SHED STICK
Your task will be much easier if a shed stick is used to make a shed in the warp threads. Use the flattened part of the shed stick and pick up alternate warp threads. **See illustration 7.** The stick should rest on the two upright bars of the frame. The warp threads are now separ-

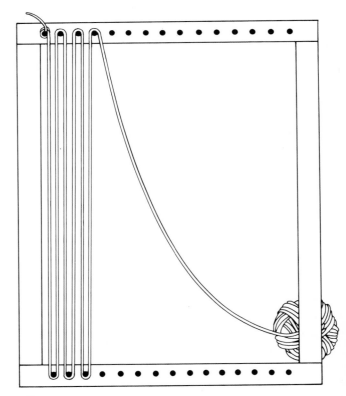

Illustration 6
Warping the frame

14

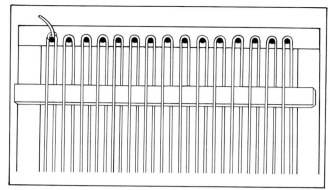

Illustration 7
Inserting the shed stick over alternating warp threads

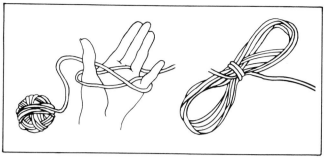

Illustration 8
A butterfly to make weaving easier

ated. This is called a shed, and this shed is called the "first shed". Every other thread lies underneath, or, to put it differently, each alternate thread lies on top of the shed stick.

The weft threads can now be woven quickly from side to side through the first shed. When the thread is woven back, the threads under the shed stick are picked up.

The frame is now prepared for weaving.

WEAVING ON THE FRAME
Before you begin, weave a small edge of about 1 cm with the warp thread. The weaving will then have a neat self-edge when it is removed from the frame.

Thread the needle with the weft thread. If the thread is too thick to go through the eye of the needle, you can make a butterfly and weave with your hand. **See illustration 8.**

Bring the needle and weft thread through the first shed. About 5 cm of the thread should remain hanging from the side. This is later woven back through the warp threads. Weave the second row by picking up the threads under the shed stick (every second thread of the warp). **See illustration 9.**

Weave the third row through the first shed, the fourth by picking up the threads underneath the shed stick, and so on.

To ensure that the sides of the weaving remain even the weft should be laid in the form of an arc or bow and then beaten down with fingers, a comb, a fork or a beater before the next row is woven. **See illustration 10.** If the arc is too small, the weaving will be pulled in. If the arc is too large, there will be unsightly loops at the edges. **See illustration 11.**

There is no prescribed size for the arc. When the weaving is wide the weft will be quite long and should therefore be laid in with a high arc. Thick, coarse and stiff wool also requires a higher arc. When the texture of

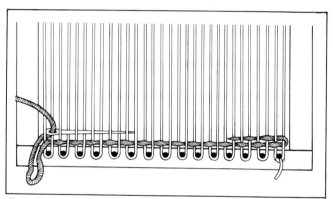

Illustration 9
Weaving with needle and weft thread

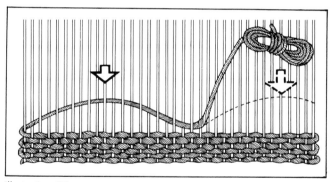

Illustration 10
The weft thread is inserted in a arc and beaten down evenly

the wool is changed, the arc should be adapted to fit the new texture. In the beginning it is difficult to maintain an even tension, but practice makes perfect. The weaving should be beaten down until the warp threads are completely covered, although when the weft threads are very thick, the warp will always be visible to some degree.

Always remember that the warp threads were origi-

15

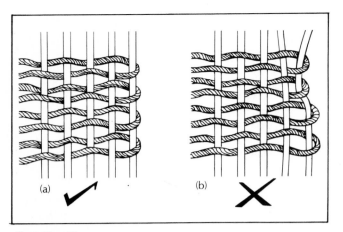

Illustration 11
(a) This weft arc is at the correct height to form a neat selvedge
(b) This weft arc is too small to form a neat selvedge; the sides of the weaving are pulled in

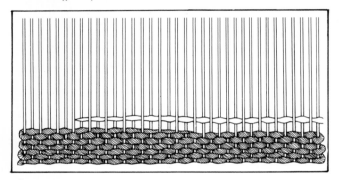

Illustration 12
Joining weft threads or changing to a new colour or texture in the weft

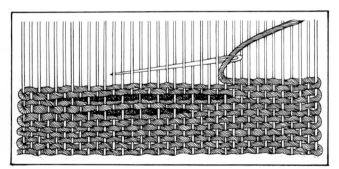

Illustration 13
Small bits of texture inlays

nally spaced 0,5 cm apart, and that this space should be maintained throughout. If the threads are pulled together or pushed out, it means that the curve of the weft thread was either too small or too large.

JOINING WEFT THREADS

When the weft threads are to be joined, the first thread is simply woven to its end. The new thread is woven over the last bit of the first thread and in the same shed. There will be a double thickness of weft threads over 4-5 cm of weaving. **See illustration 12.** As each row of weaving is beaten down, the join becomes invisible. The join will be even more inconspicuous if the thread is broken by hand, rather than cut with scissors, in order to obtain an uneven end.

With this method of joining there are no unsightly loose threads hanging down the back of the work.

HORIZONTAL CHANGES IN COLOUR AND TEXTURE

When the colours or textures of the weft threads are changed to form horizontal lines, the weft thread is woven to its end. The new colour or texture is then simply joined to the previous one in the usual way. **See illustration 12.**

A sharp horizontal distinction is obtained by first weaving with ordinary handspun wool and then changing to wool tops. Break off a piece of wool tops 20 cm longer than the width of the weaving. As wool tops is very thick, one should pull out the fibre at the ends and twist it between the fingers to form neat ends. These ends are somewhat similar to a handlebar moustache. The wool tops are laid into the first shed with a high arc leaving 5 cm protruding at each end. Fold these protrusions back round the warp into the same shed. **See photo 3.**

TEXTURE INLAYS

By adding texture inlays one can obtain interesting horizontal textural effects. Knobbly bits of mohair or wool are especially suitable for this technique. Break the strands off by hand rather than cutting them.

Weave the weft thread through. Keeping the same shed open insert textured thread of any length as long as it is shorter than the width of the article. Remember the arc. There will then be a double thickness – weft and texture – within the same shed over part of the weaving. When the weft thread is returned, the warp threads under the shed stick are picked up. **See illustration 13.** Beat the weaving down very evenly. If the textural part is very thick, it will have to be beaten down very firmly. Texture inlays should be spread evenly over the weaving, otherwise there will be a build-up of too many weft threads and inlays. **See photo 3.**

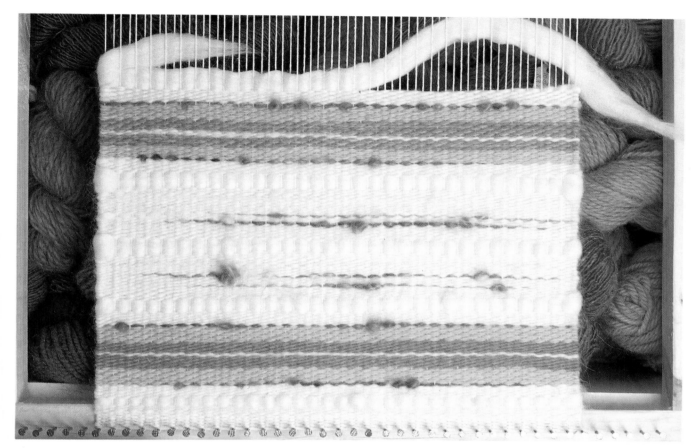

Photo 3
Very thick wool is inlayed for a horizontal texture change

JOINING COLOURS VERTICALLY

SLITS

The weft thread is usually woven across the whole width of the warp. If the weft is woven across part of the warp, turned and woven back, a slit will be formed.

This technique is used when two colours or textures are to be separated vertically by means of a slit. Decide where the slit is to be. Weave up to this point, turn, and weave backwards and forwards over this area until the required length is reached. Then weave with the second weft thread, covering the exposed area. **See illustration 14(a).**

If the slits are too long or if there are a large number of slits, the structure of the weaving will be weakened. Slits can, however, be sewn together when the weaving is complete.

If, on the other hand, there are only one or two slits, the weaving can look a bit moth eaten. Plan the placing of the slits well. **Photo 7** shows how slits were used to add dimension to the various buildings and windows in the hanging.

DOVETAILING

This technique is used to prevent slits from forming between two different colours. Weft threads of two adjacent areas are turned around a common warp thread. **See photo 4.**

Weave the first weft thread up to the point where the join is to be, turn and weave back. Weave with the second thread over the exposed area up to the last warp thread of the first colour. Turn round this warp thread, and weave back. **See illustration 14(b).**

The weft threads meet and are turned around the same warp thread. This technique results in a very neat and strong join if it is done correctly. As there will always be a ridge where the two colours are joined, one should not use this method for very long vertical lines.

STAGGERED DOVETAILING

This technique gives a neat and strong join and is suitable for long vertical lines. The weft threads do not form

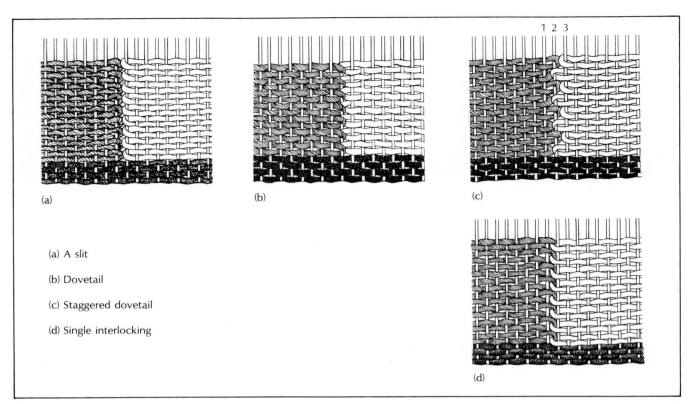

(a) A slit

(b) Dovetail

(c) Staggered dovetail

(d) Single interlocking

Illustration 14

ridges as in the previous method.

Draw a line on the warp threads where the two areas will be joined. **See illustration 14(c).** The two weft threads are woven from opposite sides up to warp threads 2 and 3, where they meet between the two warp threads, are turned and woven back. The weft threads then meet between warp threads 1 and 2. The threads again meet between warp threads 2 and 3, and so on. The threads should touch each other only lightly at each meeting. If the loops at the turns are too loose, the weaving will be rather untidy.

SINGLE INTERLOCKING
With this technique a vertical slit may be avoided. The two weft threads are woven from opposite sides to the point where the join is to be. There they are twisted around each other between two warp threads, and then each is woven back. **See illustration 14(d).**

The weft threads should not be pulled too tightly at the turn, as the warp threads will then be pulled in. If, on the other hand, the threads are too loose at the join, the weaving will have an untidy and bulky appearance.

DIAGONALS, CURVES AND CIRCLES

DIAGONALS
A technique called diagonal joining is used to form diagonal lines across the weaving. Establish the slope of the diagonal and mark this line on the warp threads. *Row 1:* Weave up to the line from right to left. *Row 2:* Weave from left to right. *Row 3:* Weave from right to left decreasing the number of warp threads by one. *Row 4:* Weave from left to right. *Row 5:* Weave from right to left again decreasing the number of warp threads by one. In this way the weaving will gradually become narrower. **See illustration 15(a).**

To cover the open area, weave from left to right to the point where the turn was made. Turn and weave back. When the third row is woven one warp thread is added to the weaving. Turn and go back. In the fifth row another warp thread is added. It is not necessary to loop the weft threads around one another, as the diagonal prevents slits from forming. The slope and the thickness of the wool will determine the tempo at which you increase or decrease the number of warp threads through

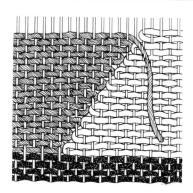

(a) Diagonal join at an angle of 45°

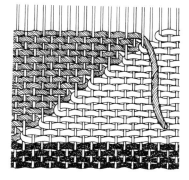

(b) Diagonal join at an angle less than 45°

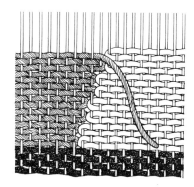

(c) Diagonal join at an angle of more than 45°

Illustration 15

which you weave. **See illustration 15(b).**

If the gradient of the line is very steep you will need to weave a few times through the same number of warp threads, and decrease this number only gradually. **See illustration 15(c).** This usually results in various small slits in the weaving.

CURVES

Decide on the size of the curve and draw it on the warp. Form the curve by weaving diagonal joins along the line of the curve, decreasing the number of warp threads according to this line. **See photos 5 and 6.** At some stage you need to decrease the number of warp threads on

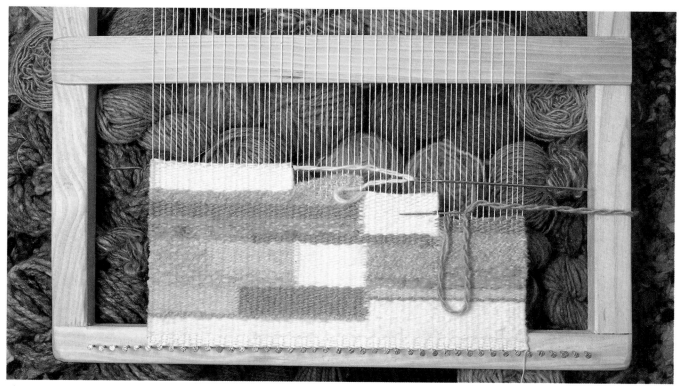

Photo 4
Vertical colour and texture divisions are obtained with dovetailing

both sides to shape the curve. **See illustration 16(a).**

The curve may be completed before the background is woven. **See illustration 16(b).**

CIRCLES

It is always better to draw the circle on to the warp before it is woven. **Illustration 17** shows the method of weaving a circle. It is important to start with the background of the lower part of the circle. **See illustration 17(a), Nos. 1** and **2.** Then the circle itself is woven. The background weaving serves as a base when the weaving of the circle is beaten down. The background is always done before the section of the circle that fits into that part of the background. In the same way the weaving shown in **illustration 17(a) No. 4** may be done in sections, but always after the relevant section of the circle has been completed.

Weaving the circumference of a circle may be compared to climbing stairs. **See illustration 17(b).** Remember that all the steps are not of the same height. The curve is formed by decreasing or increasing the number of warp threads on both sides to form the required shape.

Photo 5
Weaving a curve and making a single Ghiordes knot

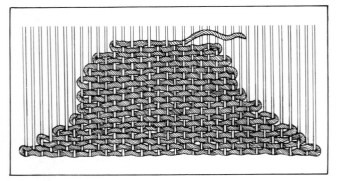

Illustration 16
(a) Weaving a curve

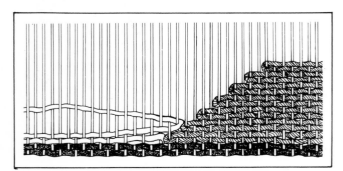

(b) Weaving the background after the curve has been completed

Photo 6
Soumak is used to outline a curve

20

Weave diagonal joins while the gradient of the circumference of the circle is not very sharp. When the gradient is nearly perpendicular you may use the dovetail technique. **See illustration 17(c).**

HATCHING

When two or more colours are joined vertically, but without a definite vertical line, the technique of hatching is used.

With this technique the colours flow together. **Projects 6** and **7** are good examples of the technique. Decide beforehand on where this technique is to be used and also whether the lines should be long, short, broad, narrow, regular or irregular.

The weft threads are woven in the same shed from opposite sides to meet at a certain point. In the next shed they return to their respective selvedges. The next meeting of the weft threads takes place at a different warp thread. **See illustration 18.**

Note that this technique must be worked row by row with both weft threads. When the two threads meet, they touch lightly between two warp threads but do not interlock.

KNOTS

WEFT LOOPING
A simple way of providing interesting textures is to pull up the weft thread so that it forms a loop on the surface.

It is best to use two weft threads, a thick as well as a thin one, so that the basic structure of the weaving remains sturdy. The thick thread or the textured one is used to form the loops, while the other one forms the background. **See illustration 19.** Weave the thin thread through the shed and beat down. Weave the thick thread through the same shed but do not beat down. Pull the loops out with a crochet hook where the weft crosses the warp. Always begin at the edge where the weft entered the shed. Weave another row with the thin thread in the second shed and beat down. This row will keep the loops firmly in place.

Both weft threads can be used to form loops, but there should always be a row of weaving between rows of loops to keep the latter in place.

The loops can be of varying lengths; they can be made over the whole row or only here and there, singly or in groups, widely spaced or against one another. They can even be used for making motifs.

These loops are used in projects 6 and 9.

GHIORDES KNOT (TURKISH KNOT, SMYRNA, RYA OR FLOSSA)
This knot is used for short pile Persian carpets as well as the traditional Scandinavian rugs which have a longer pile. The knot can be made in various ways and two methods are shown here.

Different textures can be achieved by changing the length of the pile or the number of woven rows between knotted rows.

Before experimenting with mixing colours, textures and pile lengths, you should first master the technique of making this knot.

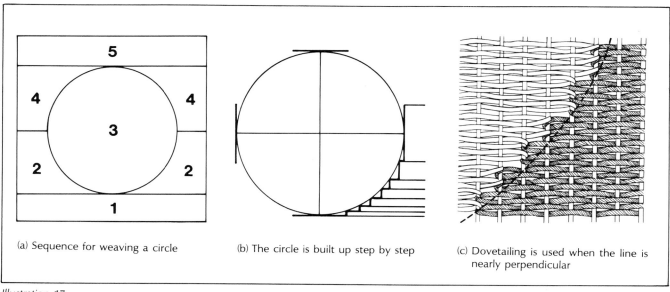

(a) Sequence for weaving a circle

(b) The circle is built up step by step

(c) Dovetailing is used when the line is nearly perpendicular

Illustration 17

21

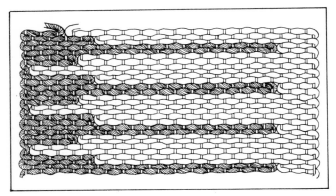

Illustration 18
Hatching

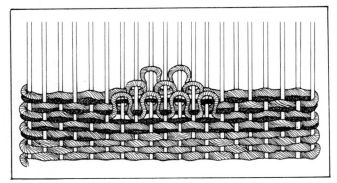

Illustration 19
Weft loops

As the Ghiordes knot can be used in many different ways, you should always plan its use within a design very thoroughly.

The Ghiordes knot is used in **projects 5, 6, 7, 9** and **10.**

Method (a): Individual knots
Cut the thread in lengths of 6-8 cm. Put one of these lengths over two warp threads. Fold the ends of the length on the outside over the two threads to the back, and then to the front between the two warp threads. Pull the knot tightly against the last row of weaving. **See illustration 20(a)** and **photo 5.** Alternate each row of knots with at least one row of weaving.

As each knot is made individually, a wide variety of effects can be achieved by changing the number of threads, the colour combination, the combinations of various textures, and the length of the pile for each knot or groups of knots.

An easy way of obtaining a single dot of colour in a piece of weaving is by making one Ghiordes knot on the required spot.

In order to work more quickly, one can cut a number of threads simultaneously.

Method (b): Knots made with one thread
Weave as usual from left to right over at least two warp threads for a neat edge.

Make the knot by taking the weft thread over and then from right to left under warp thread (i). Bring the weft over warp threads (i) and (ii). Bring the weft from right to left under warp thread (ii) so that it comes up between (i) and (ii). Tighten the knot.

At this stage the knot looks just like the one made with method (a). Use a finger to make a loop before the next one is made. **See illustration 20(b).**

The row of knots can be made over part or the whole width of the warp. Weave in the usual way through the last few warp threads to form a neat edge. Alternate each row of knots with a row of weaving.

As each loop is pulled individually, they can be of varying lengths. A wide variety of textural effects can be achieved, e.g. by not cutting the loops at all, cutting only some of the loops, cutting each loop in the middle, or cutting the loops two thirds from the end.

SOUMAK
Soumak is an oriental knot that is made by twisting the weft thread over and under the warp instead of weaving it through the warp. This knot is not part of the basic structure of the weaving, but it has a decorative function as it forms a ridge in the work. Always alternate a row of Soumak weave with at least one row of ordinary weaving. There are several variations of this knot, and the traditional knot as well as a few of the variations are shown here.

Traditional Soumak is made by taking the weft thread over four warp threads to the right and under two warp threads to the left. This constitutes one knot.

Make a row of Soumak knots by first weaving in the usual way from right to left. The Soumak knots are then made without a shed.

Take the weft thread from the left side over the first four warp threads to the right and then to the left under two warp threads. Repeat this sequence of four to the right, two underneath to the left. End the row by bringing the thread over the last four warp threads to the right. Beat the row of knots firmly down. Turn and weave in the usual way from right to left. **See illustration 21.**

A single Soumak knot is made by twisting the weft thread over and under a single warp thread. **See illustration 22.**

If there is one row of weaving throughout between the rows of knots, the ridges will all lie in the same direction.

If there are two rows of weaving between the rows of Soumak, the Soumak will lie in alternate directions. Af-

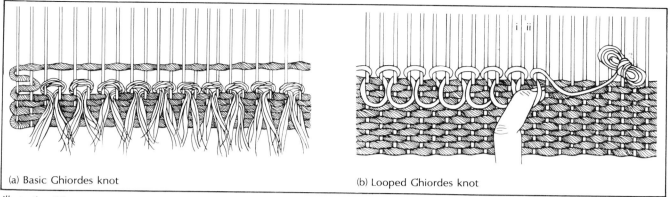

(a) Basic Ghiordes knot

(b) Looped Ghiordes knot

Illustration 20

ter the weaving has been beaten down the two rows of Soumak will form a single ridge which resembles a row of chain stitches.

For variety the number of the warp threads over and under which one weaves may be changed, as well as the thickness and texture of the weft thread.

Photo 7
Various techniques are used to obtain specific effects

23

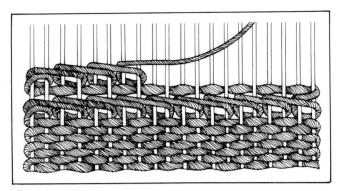

Illustration 21
Traditional Soumak

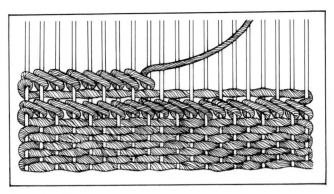

Illustration 22
Single Soumak

For a very thick ridge, two kinds of weft thread are used: a thinner one for weaving the basic structure and a very thick one for the Soumak.

Soumak need not be done over the whole width of the weaving, and may be added wherever the design requires. **See photo 7.**

One can also use Soumak for outlining curves or motifs. **See photo 6.**

Soumak is used in **projects 6**, **7**, **8** and **10**.

CHAPTER 3
Finishing off

The finishing of the article is just as important as the weaving itself and should form an integral part of your planning of the design right from the start.

If the finish is neglected or not suitable for a specific article, it will spoil the whole article and many hours of hard work will be wasted. The design of the article as well as its ultimate use will determine the choice of finish.

For runners and cushions a decorative fringe will be a good finish (**photos 22** and **23**), but in the case of the article in **photo 8** or the tray-cloth in **photo 25** it would have been inappropriate.

This chapter does not cover the whole spectrum of finishing techniques, but there should be enough ideas and variations to enable the beginner to get off to a good start.

As you gain experience you will also gain the confidence to try out new and original methods of finishing your work.

REMOVING THE WEAVING FROM THE FRAME

Weaving can be removed from the frame in two ways depending on whether the whole area of the warp has been covered or only a part of it. **See illustrations 23(a) and (b).** Make sure that all alterations are completed before the work is removed from the frame.

Method (a)
When you weave right up to the top nails, the top and bottom edges will form self-edges and less time needs to be spent on finishing.

Weaving the last few centimetres requires some extra care and time, as the space through which you can weave becomes smaller and smaller.

When you have woven to about 5-10 cm from the top, you can use a double thickness of warp thread as weft to weave an edge against the nails. Beat this up to the nails. Then weave the last few centimetres between the edge and the weaving. Do this carefully, as there is

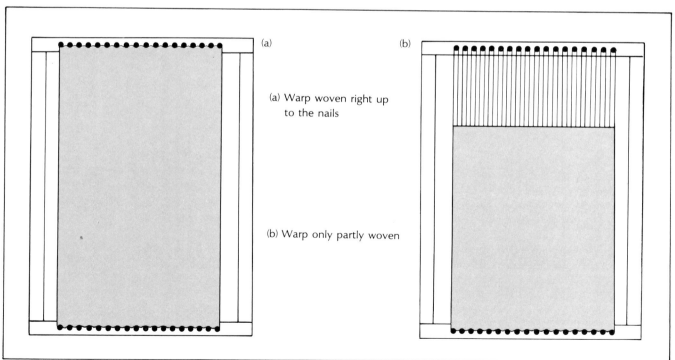

(a)
(b)

(a) Warp woven right up to the nails

(b) Warp only partly woven

Illustration 23

Photo 8
Wall hanging by Elna de Kock. This wall hanging was finished with a tube sewn to the back of the weaving. A rod was inserted. Further finishing would be unnecessary and could easily spoil the effect of the weaving

very little space in which to work. Using a shorter needle, such as a thick darning needle, helps, as well as weaving through short areas at a time.

When the warp is completely covered, the knots where the warp has been tied to the nails at the top and bottom are loosened. Insert the point of a darning needle in the knot and loosen. **See illustration 24.**

The work can now be unhooked from the nails with a crochet hook. **See illustration 25.** Unhook the work alternatively from top and bottom nails. Sew loose threads into the edges. Edges may be folded over and sewn with hem stitch to the back. **See illustration 26.**

Method (b)
If you do not weave right up to the nails, leave enough of the warp to enable you to knot these loose ends easily. You need at least 5 cm lengths of warp threads

for cutting and tying knots.

Remember to finish with a 1 cm woven edge at the top. Check the whole length of your work to ensure that the tension is the same throughout. The length of the work may be corrected by beating down where necessary.

Cut off two warp threads at a time and knot them together. The knot should just touch the top edge.

Continue in this way until all the warp threads have been cut off. **See illustration 27.** Loosen the knot around the nail at the bottom of the frame by prying it loose with a darning needle. **See illustration 24.** Use a crochet hook to remove the work from the nails. The loose threads at the bottom of the weaving are worked back into the edge.

Loose warp threads at the top of the work can also be sewn into the weaving. **See illustration 28.** Edges can be finished off with hem stitch. **See illustration 26.**

ADDING A FRINGE

You need not add fringes to all your work. Some articles such as runners and cushions, do, however, look better with a fringe.

The fringe need not be of the same length throughout. Varying lengths of fringe are very effective. **See photos 16** and **30.** The fringe need not always be made from cotton, wool or mohair, and strips of leather, raffia or string can provide a very interesting finish.

There are many methods of making fringes, two are shown here. **See illustrations 29(a)** and **(b).**

Another method of making a fringe is shown in **project 4.**

Method (a)
Decide on the length of the fringe. Cut the thread so that it is twice the length of the fringe plus a few centimetres for the knot.

The number of threads in each fringe depends on the thickness of the thread used in the fringe. If ordinary handspun wool or mohair is used, three threads will suffice, but if the thread is very thin, use more threads.

If the fringe is knotted over the hemmed edge a neat and well-finished effect is obtained.

Fold the required number of threads in half. Insert a crochet hook from the back of the weaving to the front, loop the threads and pull to the back of the weaving. Tie the fringe to the weaving by pulling the loose threads through the loop at the back, and pulling it against the weaving. **See illustration 29(a).**

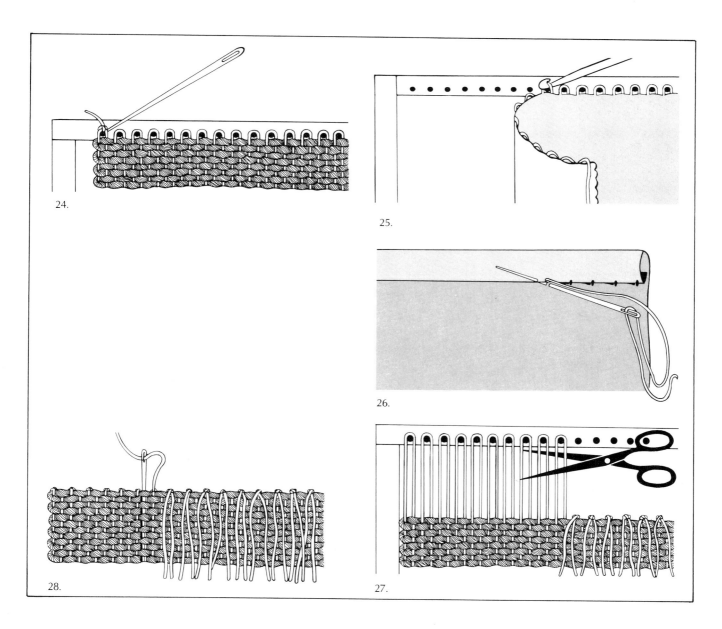

24.

25.

26.

28.

27.

Method (b)
Alternatively half of the required number of threads are pulled through the weaving to the back just above the hemmed edge with a crochet hook. Tie the fringe to the weaving by making an overhand knot. **See illustration 29(b).**

The knots of the fringes should be spaced so that they lightly touch one another.

IDEAS FOR FINISHING WALL-HANGINGS

There are many ways of finishing wall-hangings. The ideas given here will serve as a starting point from which to work and with which to experiment.

The projects in this book illustrate a wide variety of ways in which to finish woven articles.

The beginner should study these projects and pay special attention to the methods of finishing. It is also possible that the weaver might not like one of the given methods, and may decide to devise her own. This will be a big step forward indeed!

One of the projects **(photo 28)** is framed, while another one remains stretched in a frame **(photo 29)**. These methods are not described here, so as to inspire the weaver to try other and more interesting ways to suspend wall hangings.

The finishing should always fit in with the theme or idea of the weaving. For example, a hanging with an

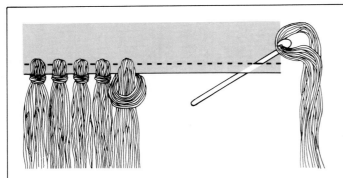

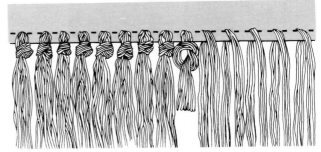

(a) To tie a knot, the fringe is pulled through the weaving with a crochet hook

(b) The fringe is tied with an overhand knot over the seam

ethnic theme is hung on a knobkerrie. **See photo 16.** The hanging with reeds and bamboo, on the other hand, hangs from a large bamboo rod. **See photo 32.** Sometimes loops and/or rods at the top and fringes at the bottom are quite unnecessary. **See photo 8.** This hanging is so striking that any further embellishments will only detract from the overall effect.

MOUNTING ON HESSIAN
An easy but striking way to finish off a woven hanging is by mounting it on hessian. Sew it on to a piece of hessian, and stretch it over a panel of pressed wood. **See illustration 30(a).** The advantage of this method is that the end product is always larger than the weaving itself. **See photo 9.** Remember that the colour of the hessian should blend in with or complement the colour of the weaving.

Measure the length and breadth of the weaving after the seams have been worked. Decide on the measurements of the hessian. If the weaving is 50 cm × 50 cm, and the hessian is to be 7 cm wide on all sides, the pressed wood board should be 64 cm × 64 cm. Add 10 cm to this length and breadth to calculate the size of the hessian. The hessian then measures 74 cm × 74 cm. The extra 10 cm is needed for stretching the hessian on the board.

Zigzag the edges of the hessian as it frays easily. Place the weaving carefully in the middle of the hessian and sew it to the hessian. Place the hessian on the panel so that the weaving lies in the middle, and fold in the corners. Sew the horizontal sides together, and then the vertical sides. See **illustration 30(b).** For a neat background, a piece of brown paper (somewhat smaller than the board) can be glued over the threads with cold glue.

ROD THROUGH THE WARP THREADS
The weaving can also be made to hang on a rod inserted in the warp threads at the top. **See illustration 31.**

This method can only be used if the warp threads at the top are long enough to fit over the rod, bamboo or knobkerrie. **See photo 32.** This should be taken into account when the size of the frame and weaving is planned in the beginning. An extra length of about 5 cm is needed for the warp threads.

When the weaving has been completed, an edge of 2 or 3 rows are woven with flax instead of an edge of 1 cm. Finish on the left of the weaving with a long string of flax (three times the breadth of the weaving). Sew overhand stitches from left to right. **See illustration 32.** Use a darning needle for this. Then loosen the warp thread around the top nails. Unhook the warp from the nails with a crochet hook, give it a twist, and insert the rod. The loose warp thread at the end can be twisted around the rod to form a loop, and the end can then be sewn into the edge. The rest of the finishing is done in the usual way.

WOVEN LOOPS
A rod can also be inserted through woven loops at the top of the weaving. **See photos 20** and **21.**

If there is sufficient warp on the frame, the loops can be woven directly on to the weaving, or they can be woven separately. The loops need not always be woven, but can be made from strips of leather and simply sewn on to the weaving. **See photo 16.** Before the loops are woven or made, it is important to decide on the length and width of each loop, the number required and their colour.

It is a great help to draw the loops on a piece of paper and cut them out. Fold the paper loop in half and place

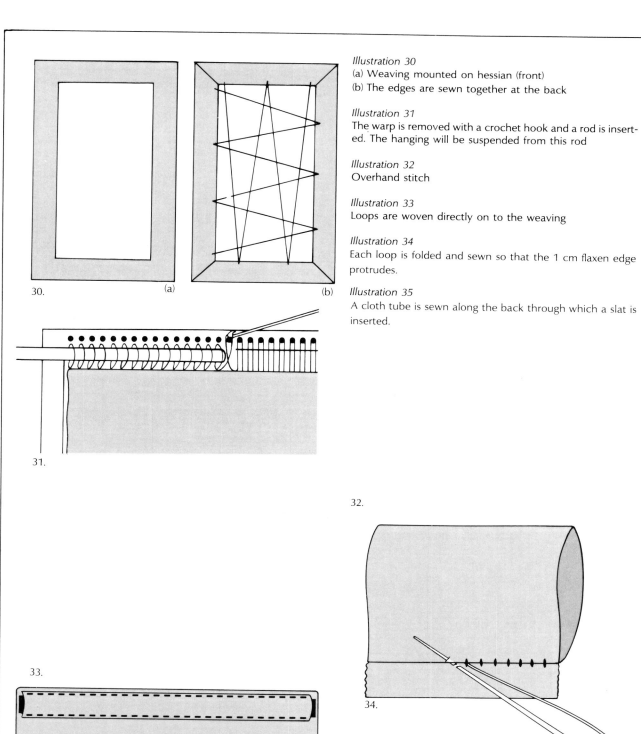

Illustration 30
(a) Weaving mounted on hessian (front)
(b) The edges are sewn together at the back

Illustration 31
The warp is removed with a crochet hook and a rod is inserted. The hanging will be suspended from this rod

Illustration 32
Overhand stitch

Illustration 33
Loops are woven directly on to the weaving

Illustration 34
Each loop is folded and sewn so that the 1 cm flaxen edge
protrudes.

Illustration 35
A cloth tube is sewn along the back through which a slat is
inserted.

30.

(a)

(b)

31.

32.

33.

34.

35.

Photo 9
Weaving by Claudine Louw mounted on hessian

it on the top edge of the weaving. This will give you an idea whether they are the right size or not.

LOOPS WOVEN ON TO THE WEAVING

If the loops are going to be woven directly on to the weaving, the 1 cm edge should not be completed. Arrange the paper loops above the article to check the spacing. Each final loop is then woven separately over the required number of warp threads. **See illustration 33.**

When a loop has been completed, an edge of 1 cm can be woven with flax at the top of the loop. Each loop will therefore have its own woven edge.

Edges of 1 cm each are also woven on the warp threads between the loops. There should be a slit between each loop and this edge. Remove the weaving from the frame and sew loose threads in according to method (b) in this chapter.

After all the loose threads have been sewn in, the loops are folded over so that the 1 cm flax edge lies against the top of the weaving. Baste. The 1 cm edges between loops are also folded back and basted to the back of the weaving. Now there should be a continuous edge at the back. Sew this edge to the weaving. Insert the rod through the loops.

LOOPS WOVEN SEPARATELY

If there is not enough warp left on which to weave the loops, they can be woven separately.

If five loops, each one 5 cm wide, are needed, five separate sets of warp threads are threaded, each one over 6 nails. Each loop is then woven. When the loop is completed, an edge of 1 cm is woven with flax. Each loop has its own edge. The loops are removed from the frame and loose threads sewn in. Fold the loop so that the 1 cm flaxen edge protrudes at the bottom and sew the woven edges together. **See illustration 34.**

Sew the 1 cm flaxen edge to the flaxen edge of the weaving. Insert the rod.

Photo 10
Weaving by Elsabé Toua. The fringe is incorporated within the design by knotting the fringe on part of the design only

A SLAT AT THE BACK OF THE WEAVING

Sometimes the loops, warp threads or rods at the top of the weaving are unnecessary. The weaving is simply finished at the top and a cloth tube is sewn along the back, through which a slat is inserted. **See illustration 35 and photos 8 and 10.**

CHAPTER 4

Inspiration and design

Every human being is creative and wants to create. However, when words such as **inspiration, creativity or design** are mentioned, many people feel threatened and cannot associate themselves with these attributes. The words are moreover often bandied about without their full meaning being realized. This is due to the fact that the creative part of children's make-up is neglected and hampered by today's educational systems.

Weavers are often put off by the idea of designing their own articles, and therefore they tend to copy existing designs over and over. It is a safe option and at least they are then sure of the results.

It is a good idea for the beginner to learn by using existing designs. In this way you can concentrate on mastering the new techniques. As you become more experienced you should, however, learn to study the work of other weavers to evaluate them and to be inspired by them to create your own designs.

Each one of us has some creative talents. And one's creativity can be compared to the working of muscles: the more they are exercised, the better they function.

Your creative abilities, together with **inspiration, enthusiasm** and **imagination** can be used to design your own weaving patterns.

Basic design may be approached in various ways. In this chapter the matter of design will be compared to birth. A birth can only occur if conception and development of the fetus have taken place. The following comparison can be made:

- Inspiration — conception
- Development of the creative ideas — development of the fetus
- Design — birth

A few basic ideas on inspiration, creativity and design will be dealt with in the hope that you will be inspired to such an extent that you begin to develop your own designs and so put a personal stamp on your work.

INSPIRATION

It has been said that genius is 1% inspiration and 99% perspiration.

Inspiration is the spontaneous impulse that sets the creative process in motion. The creative process is a necessary part of designing. Inspiration is an involuntary, spontaneous reaction and does not always happen on demand.

You can, however, prepare the ground for inspiration by looking honestly at yourself and deciding on your priorities. You should try to ascertain what makes you happy as a person, what your likes and dislikes are, and what aspects of life you find most meaningful.

Factors such as differences in education, experience, environment and relationships will all determine each person's individual interests.

The next step is to develop and stimulate your interest in nature, colour, texture, emotion and form, until an intense awareness grows from this. This in turn will lead

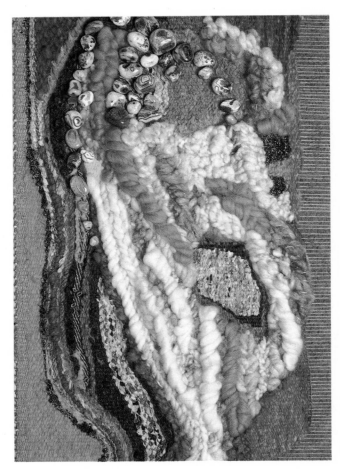

Photo 11
Incomplete work by Wilma Besselson. The lines and colours of an agate served as inspiration for this work

32

to the forming of unique ideas on the subject, which will lead to inspiration.

Interest
(nature and textures)

Intense awareness
(see/experience nature and textures with new eyes)

Inspiration
(spontaneous reaction to e.g. a striking silhouette of a tree)

Photo 12
The inspiration for this incomplete weaving by Claudine Louw was the shape and colour of a Venus's-ear shell

SOURCES OF INSPIRATION

The world around us is a never-ending source of inspiration. And yet, because of the technological developments of the past few decades and the restless hurry-scurry of everyday life, we have become alienated from many of the art forms in nature, such as driftwood, pebbles, seeds and rocks.

For inspiration to succeed, we have to form a deep and lasting friendship with the earth. We have to learn to look with new awareness and interest at the amazing variety of forms, lines, textures and colours which surround us and which sometimes appear in the most unexpected places.

Here are some ideas which may serve as a starting point for inspiration:

● the colours of a sunrise, a sunset, autumn leaves, fields of wild flowers, scales on a fish;
● the shape of seeds, leaves, stones, trees, flowers;
● the textures of bark, weathered old buildings, freshly ploughed fields, satin;
● the lines formed by wrinkles in a face, dried and cracked mud, sand-dunes in the desert, the face of a krans, growth rings in a tree trunk;

Photo 13
"Crow's nest" by Elsabé Toua was developed after the crow's nest and stick were picked up on the beach. It was built around the colours of the crow's nest

Photo 14
The colours and rectangular shapes on the cushion and runner woven by Claudine Louw were inspired by blocks of wood

- children's drawings, sketches;
- the man-made forms of buildings and roads, architectural forms;
- symbolic forms such as circles, crosses, stars.

In this way the lines and colours of pebbles were the source of inspiration of the weaving in **photo 11**.

The curve of a Venus-ear shell and the colours on the inside of the shell were the starting point of the weaving in **photo 12**.

The crow's nest in **photo 13** was picked up on the beach and inspired the weaver to design a work based on the colours of the mixture of seaweed and strings.

The various lines, shapes and shades obtained when pieces of wood are stacked were the inspiration for the design and colour of the runner and cushion in **photo 14**.

Not one of these weavings is a duplication of nature. They serve as an example of how the individual can be inspired by nature and interpret this in a unique way. You should not concentrate on a specific source of inspiration, but try to find those elements which can be utilized and interpreted so that the article will be an expression of your own personality.

An idea originates from somewhere (conception takes place), and the creative process is set in motion (the fetus begins to develop). What will help this process along?

THE CREATIVE PROCESS

Creativity is necessary if one wants to design. The creative process is put in motion by inspiration, and can be developed, by **imagination**, to grow into a basic design (the creative product). After conception the fetus starts to develop. Some factors are necessary for healthy growth.

During the growth process we react to inspiration by becoming intensely aware of it. In practice that means that we not only **look**, but we **see**; we not only **touch**, but **feel**. We reach more deeply than the surface. We need to spend time looking at our source of inspiration with an open and receptive mind, in order to see, to experience, to explore.

For example, use a tree as a source of inspiration. **See illustration 36**. If you look at it from a distance, the tree may be part of other trees in a wood or copse. As you approach, the form of the tree becomes clearer. It is big, with wide branches. If you look closer still, the leaves and twigs become distinguishable. You can see, and feel, cracks and fissures in the bark, the form and veins of the leaves, the lines of the branches. It may be an old

oak tree with a hollow trunk, so that you can look inside it, smell it and experience it. Leaves and parts of the bark can be studied under a microscope.

Sit under the tree, climb into the tree and look at the tree from the top by climbing a ladder. What does the tree look like at sunrise and sunset, in the moonlight, when it rains, when the wind blows?

Try to make sketches of ideas that emerge during this process.

While one is so intensely **aware**, the imagination interprets the inspiration in terms of **line, form, texture** and **colour** (these are all elements of design), in order to find a possible design.

Use your creative abilities to interpret your personal discoveries and experiences regarding, for instance, a tree and to evolve them into a basic design which will be an **extension** of your own **personality**. (The fetus is developing and healthy.)

During this process of growth you should be as receptive as possible and not critical at all. Try to develop different possibilities; this will ensure a greater chance of success. Allow the growth process to develop at its own pace. (Avoid induction and allow the birth to take place as naturally as possible.)

The growth process can continue until the point is reached where a specific sketch is preferred to the others, feels more important and is of greater value than the others.

The design is now in its initial stage, and can be analysed critically according to the principles of good design. (Birth has taken place and the newborn is inspected critically to make sure that everything is normal.)

BASIC DESIGN

Basic design is the combination of **lines, shapes, textures** and **colours** in an area. These are called the **elements** of design and in a broad sense, they constitute the building materials for design.

The success of a design is determined by the way in which the various elements are combined. This, in turn, is determined by the **principles** of **balance, focal point, proportion** and **rhythm.**

The elements and basic principles of design are discussed, not to lay down rules for design, but to bring them to the attention of the beginner and to assist her in making her own designs.

The elements and principles are discussed separately, but it should always be borne in mind that each element and principle is connected to all the others in some way.

ELEMENTS OF DESIGN

Together with inspiration and creative thinking the elements of design, namely **line, shape, texture** and **colour**, can serve as building materials for the basic design of a woven article. Each of these elements is to be found in nature as well as in man-made objects.

Line

A line is the shortest distance between two points. It certainly is the simplest of all the elements and yet it has endless possibilities. A line may be thick, thin, uneven, curved, horizontal, diagonal, vertical, short or long, to name only a few. **See illustration 37.** In weaving the

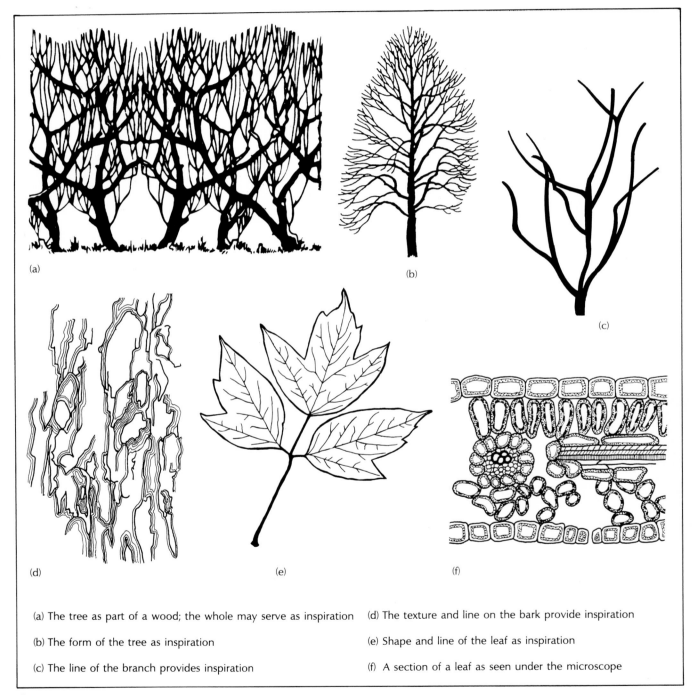

(a)

(b)

(c)

(d)

(e)

(f)

(a) The tree as part of a wood; the whole may serve as inspiration

(b) The form of the tree as inspiration

(c) The line of the branch provides inspiration

(d) The texture and line on the bark provide inspiration

(e) Shape and line of the leaf as inspiration

(f) A section of a leaf as seen under the microscope

Illustration 36

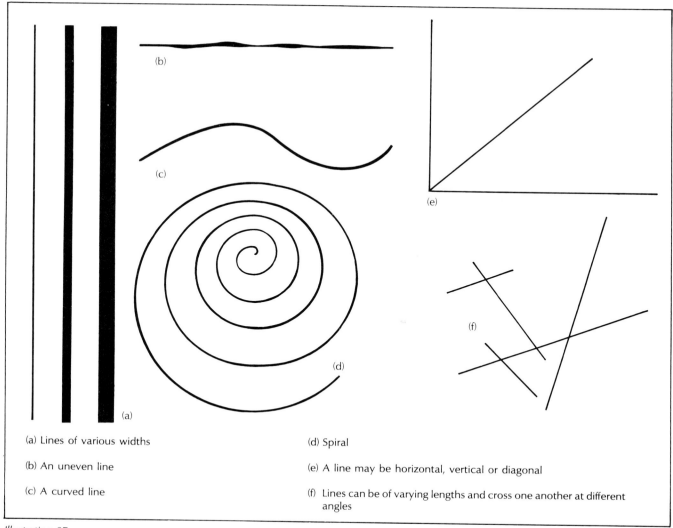

(a) Lines of various widths

(b) An uneven line

(c) A curved line

(d) Spiral

(e) A line may be horizontal, vertical or diagonal

(f) Lines can be of varying lengths and cross one another at different angles

Illustration 37

quality of a line will vary according to the texture of the weft threads.

A line draws the eye in various directions and can convey a feeling of movement, whether fast or rhythmical. Line can be used as a form of expression; it can convey a certain feeling and can create atmosphere.

Lines can be seen even when they are not really there. The eye connects small objects that are similar, and this then has the effect of a line. **See illustration 38(a).**

Horizontal lines cause an object to appear broader and vertical lines make it appear longer than it really is. **See illustration 38(b).** In **illustration 38(c)** horizontal lines are used to create an illusion of distance. By placing the horizontal lines nearer to one another as they go upward, an illusion of space is created.

In nature, lines may be observed in rock formations, in the grain of wood, the horizon, the veins of a leaf, feathers, branches or a spider's web.

In weaving, lines are an integral part of the structure (warp and weft), as well as the visual design. It is therefore an important element of weaving. **See photo 15.**

Shape
The outline of an area is its shape. The area within the outline is the positive shape, while the area outside the line is the negative shape. **See illustration 39(a).** Both these shapes need to be taken into account when shape is an element of the design. Like a line, the shape of an area has various properties. It can be realistic or abstract, and an abstract shape can be geometric, organic or uneven.

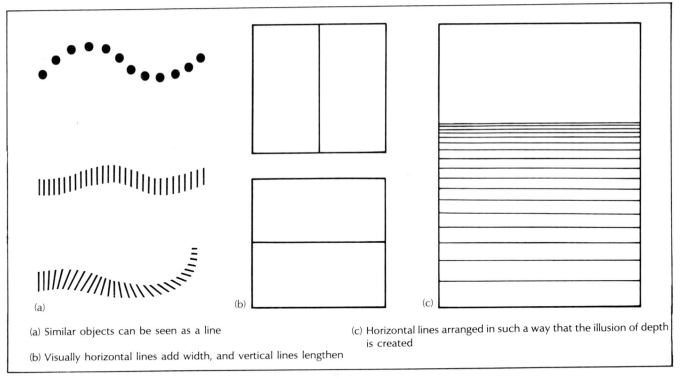

(a) Similar objects can be seen as a line

(b) Visually horizontal lines add width, and vertical lines lengthen

(c) Horizontal lines arranged in such a way that the illusion of depth is created

Illustration 38

Shapes differ in size and complexity and can also be connected to other shapes. **See illustration 39(b).**

In nature, there are simple shapes such as pebbles, and complicated ones such as mountain ranges.

In weaving, shapes are created by colours, different textures or techniques. **See photo 16.** As you use more and more shapes, the opportunities for developing the basic design can be increased considerably.

Texture
Texture is the quality of the surface of an object. We observe texture with our tactile sense, but we also experience it visually, because we know – by sight – what a specific texture feels like.

Nature provides us with an endless number of textures. Think, for example, of the rough bark of a tree and the spongy lichen on that bark, a prickly pear leaf, a satiny rose-leaf, a smooth pebble and the fur of an angora rabbit.

Texture and weaving are completely integrated. Weaving is texture, whether it is fine and smooth or coarse and chunky. Even when one weaves with only one kind of thread, one has texture. Variety is achieved by changing one's technique of weaving, the colour or the quality of the thread.

By changing the texture of the weaving lines, shapes and also various colour tones can be created. A very

definite texture will also give real dimension to the surface. **See photo 17.** The only danger is to overdo the use of texture. It is very easy to become quite carried away

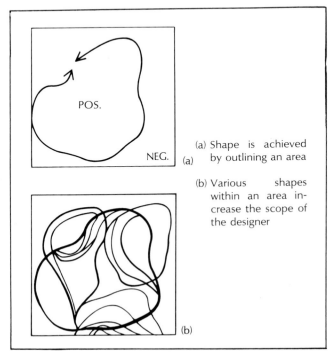

(a) Shape is achieved by outlining an area

(b) Various shapes within an area increase the scope of the designer

Illustration 39

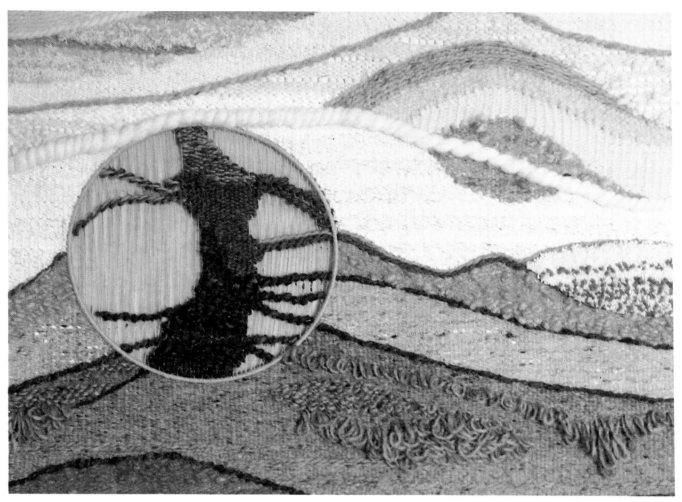

Photo 15
Weaving by Anella Gerber where the design was built around various lines

by the many and various kinds of texture available to the weaver.

The texture should always suit the design. The texture of the threads, the weaving structure and the colour should all complement the design and form a harmonious whole.

Colour

Colour is a very important part of the weaving design. Some of the principles involved may be of help to the beginner, as long as one realizes that there are no hard and fast rules.

Every colour has the following characteristics:
• shade – the name of the colour, such as blue or green
• tone – light or dark
• intensity – bright or dull.

These characteristics are used to describe a colour in the same way that height, breadth and depth describe an object. In this way we can talk about a dull dark blue, or a light bright red.

The colour wheel has twelve colours. **See illustration 40.** Colours are classified according to their position on the colour wheel.
• The primary colours of red, yellow and blue are the colours from which all other colours are composed.
• Secondary colours are green, orange and purple. They are obtained when equal amounts of two primary colours are mixed. Yellow and blue give green, red and yellow give orange, and blue and red give purple.
• Tertiary colours are colours such as blue-green, and are obtained by mixing a primary colour with a secondary colour.

Two colours directly opposite each other on the colour wheel, such as yellow and purple, are complementary colours. As there is a very strong contrast between these colours, they should not be used in equal amounts in a design. A very striking effect is

Photo 16
In this weaving by Esmé Theron, organic forms were used to develop the design

achieved when one colour dominates and a little bit of the complementary colour is added. An example of complementary colours in nature is the sun and the sky. If the sun is bright, the sky and the sea seem very blue.

Black and white are neutral colours. They provide a colour with its tone. If white is added, colours become lighter; black makes them darker. Black and white give lighter or darker shades of a colour, but they cannot change the intensity of the colour.

You do not weave an article in order to put it away in a drawer. When choosing the colours of the design, you should also take into account the colour scheme of the room where the article is to be used. Remember that the character of a colour is changed by the colour used in conjunction with it. The human eye sees colour relative to other colours.

Colours such as red, orange and yellow give a feeling of warmth and excitement, while blue, purple and green have a cool, calm and restful effect.

A colour will appear to be darker and deeper if used with white, while colours used with black will seem lighter and brighter. When various colours of high intensity are used together, the brightest colour will appear brighter and the dullest colour will appear even duller. The intensity of the brightest colours is softened by using neutral or dull colours in the design.

Colours from the same area on the colour wheel work well together and give a subtle and satisfying overall effect. Soft pink and light mauve or lilac are examples of such harmonising colours.

A very dramatic effect can be achieved with complementary colours. There is a sharp contrast between these colours and they should not be used in equal amounts. If one of the colours dominates, and only a small amount of the complementary colour is used, this will have a very vibrant effect.

The texture of the thread should also be considered when colours are chosen. A shiny thread always looks brighter than a hairy thread. The texture obtained by a specific technique also has an effect on the colours. Coarse surface textures will form shadows and hollows in the weaving, and the colours will therefore appear deeper and richer.

The aspirant weaver, who may be somewhat unsure about the use of colours, will do well to limit the use of colour in her work at first.

BASIC PRINCIPLES OF DESIGN
Basic principles of design are **guide-lines** for the use and arrangement of the building materials of design, (elements of design). A few of the most important principles – **balance, focal point, proportion** and **rhythm** – are discussed here.

Balance
A design is well balanced when it appears **visually balanced**. Although balance can be formal or informal, only the latter kind falls within the scope of this book.

Informal balance is used in free or asymmetrical designs. The elements of an asymmetrical design should give a visual feeling of balance. A small element can have as much visual weight as a bigger one, if the smaller element is richer in texture, brighter in colour or has a more interesting shape.

Good design is the perfect balance between **uniformity** (oneness, order) and **variety.** Uniformity means that

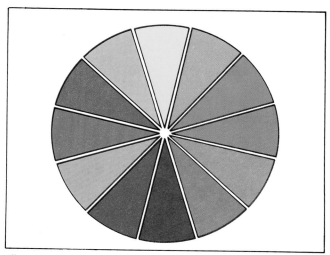

Illustration 40
The colour wheel

the elements of the design such as the colour, line and texture are ordered and used in such a way that the whole satisfies the brain's striving for order. However, variety is also important. If the object that the eye sees is interesting, the brain is stimulated to continue to observe.

Be careful of too much variety in a design, such as contrast in colour, shape and texture. This can have a chaotic effect.

Uniformity is achieved by basing the design on one shape and colour. Variety is achieved by changing the size of the shapes, and the texture and tonal quality of the colour. **See photo 19.**

Focal point
The focal point is that point in the design which is **noticed first of all**, the point to which the eye tends to return. Effective designs usually have focal points. A stone thrown through a window is a good example of a focal point. One first notices the point where the stone hit the window; the eye moves to other areas, but returns to the first point.

When we look at something, our eyes are inclined to come to rest at a position slightly higher than and to the left of the centre of the area. This then is the natural area to place a focal point. This does not mean that the focal point has to be there. But if the focal point is moved from this natural point to, say, the right and underneath the centre, the rest of the design has to be adapted to this to get a balanced effect for the total design. **See photo 19.**

A focal point can be achieved in various ways. A specific shape can be used in a design, and a more

Photo 17
In this weaving by Wilma Besselson, textures were used to suggest an under-water scene

complicated version can then form the focal point.

One's attention is also drawn by contrasts in colour or texture. Contrast that is achieved by means of colour, texture, line or shape should, however, be used with discretion.

There can be more than one focal point as long as these do not carry equal weight in the design, otherwise the eyes will continually move from the one to the other and be unable to come to rest. Try to achieve one main focal point and a few less important ones. They should

Photo 18
Weaving in primary colours by Elsabé Warren

43

Photo 19
This weaving by Claudine Louw demonstrates balance and a focal point

be arranged in such a way that the eyes travel naturally from the most important one to the least important one.

Rhythm

Rhythm in a design is achieved when a line or shape creates a feeling of **visual movement.** The design is then composed in such a way that the eyes travel easily from one line to another, or from one shape to another.

Think again about the stone thrown through a window. From the focal point – where the stone hit the window – the eyes travel quickly and rhythmically along the cracks. A stone thrown in a pool of water also results in rhythmical movement.

Repetition of lines, colours, shapes or textures brings about a feeling of rhythm if the principle of uniformity is applied at the same time. Repetition of one shape for instance can easily become monotonous. Repeat the same shape in a design, but allow it to grow and shrink within the design. The repetition of lines and the result-

Photo 20
In this weaving by Petro Smit, rhythm is achieved through repetition

ing rhythmic effect is clearly seen in **photo 20.** Here monotony is prevented by changing the colours.

Proportion
In a good design all the parts should be arranged in such a way that their proportions to one another, within the design, are satisfactory.

This principle of design has to do with the planning and organising of the kinds of shapes, their size and their arrangement within the area so that the design becomes well balanced as a whole. **See photo 21.**

When the kind and size of the shapes are planned, it is important to remember that the eye sees objects in their relation to other objects. If an object is compared to a large one, it will seem small, but that same object will seem large if compared to a smaller one. A thin line seems even thinner when compared to a very heavy one.

Try not to disrupt the proportion of a design by placing a very large shape next to a small one, or by using a geometric shape with organic shapes. A specific part of a design may appear correct when seen on its own, but be completely out of proportion to the rest of the design.

Visualise the various parts of the design in relation to the whole in order to apply the principle of proportion.

45

Photo 21
"Township" by Wiebke Lusted illustrates a good balance between line/shape and colour

CONCLUSION

The purpose of this chapter is to help the beginner with the process of design. The basic information has been given. The way in which this information is received and the extent to which the information will be used, are in the hands of the aspiring designer.

Hopefully the seeds have been sown and creative frame-weaving will prove to be a fruitful medium for the development of the process of designing.

Runner

RUNNER

This project is simple, yet striking. It is ideal for the beginner as one weaves in horizontal lines only. Variety is achieved by using different colours and textures and by texture inlays.

The purpose of this project is to teach the basic technique of weaving, as well as the technique for changing from one weft thread to another. Interest is added by using a very simple technique, that of texture inlays.

Those who feel more daring need not use the pattern given in the diagram, but use their own combinations of colours and lines.

SIZE
Width:
30 cm
Length:
40 cm without fringe
60 cm with fringe

MATERIALS
Frame:
Frame 1
Warp:
50 g $\frac{8}{12}$ 100% cotton or any other strong 100% cotton thread
Weft:

100 g cream wool ⎤
25 g light pink wool ⎬ Wool should be as thick as ordinary double knit wool
25 g dark pink wool ⎦
50 g cream wool tops
remnants of textured wool (green and pink)
Fringe:
50 g cream mohair (thin and handspun)

METHOD
Thread the warp over 31 nails, using 100% cotton. Weave an edge of about 1 cm using a double thickness of cotton.

When the edge has been completed, weave with the wool in the sequence given in **illustration 41**. **Photo 3** shows the technique of inlaying the wool tops, and **illustration 13** shows how to do the texture inlays.

Note: If you are a beginner, you should check the width of the weaving after every few rows of weaving. If the web is wider or narrower than 30 cm, it means that you have made a mistake regarding the height of the arc. Unravel and start again. But do not despair! Once you have mastered this technique, it will become second nature.

FINISHING
When the 1 cm cotton edge has been completed, the length of the weaving must be checked before it is cut off.

Measure the length of the weaving at the sides and in the centre. When the cotton edge is added, the length should be 42 cm throughout. If the length is irregular, the web should be beaten down until the weaving is completely rectangular.

Warp threads are then cut off two at a time and about 5 cm from the cotton edge. Tie the threads twice (with an ordinary knot) against the weaving. Continue in this way until all the threads have been cut off and tied.

The knot around the nail at the bottom of the frame can now be loosened. Loop the weaving from the nails with a crochet hook. Fold the ends back and sew to the front.

FRINGE
Cut the mohair in lengths of 24 cm. Use three strands at a time and loop it with the crochet hook through the weaving just above the edge, as shown in **illustration 29(b)**. Tie each group of threads with an overhand knot. The fringe should be spaced evenly.

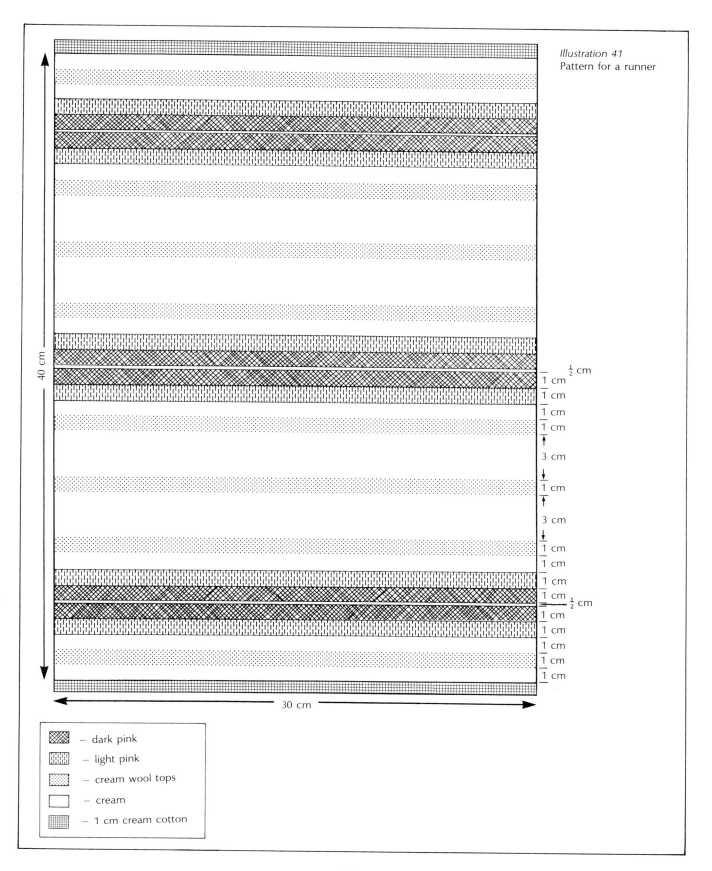

Illustration 41
Pattern for a runner

½ cm
1 cm
1 cm
1 cm
1 cm
3 cm
1 cm
3 cm
1 cm
1 cm
1 cm
1 cm ½ cm
1 cm
1 cm
1 cm
1 cm
1 cm

40 cm

30 cm

▨	– dark pink
▦	– light pink
▨	– cream wool tops
☐	– cream
▦	– 1 cm cream cotton

Photo 22
A variety of runners and cushions woven by members of the Kuil's River branch of the WAA

Cushion cover

CUSHION COVER

The weaver has now mastered the basic weaving techniques and the technique for maintaining the correct tension, and is ready to practise one or two new ones.

In this project rectangles of various sizes are used to enable the beginner to practise the techniques of dovetailing, staggered dovetailing, and interlocking.

These techniques need not necessarily be practised on a cushion cover. This project can also be used as a runner. The colours and the size of the rectangles can also be changed to suit the taste of the weaver. The illustration serves merely as an aid for those who want to work from a pattern.

Do not hesitate to use your own colour scheme and design of rectangles. It is most enjoyable to weave each rectangle with a new colour or new texture. So relax and enjoy the experience of weaving!

SIZE
Width:
35 cm without fringe
50 cm with fringe
Length:
32,5 cm without fringe
47,5 cm with fringe

MATERIALS
Frame:
Frame 1
Warp:
50 g $\frac{8}{12}$ 100% cotton or any other strong 100% cotton
Weft:
250 g light cream (main colour)
 25 g each of light, medium and dark beige
 25 g each of beige and rust coloured bouclé wool
Fringe:
50 g mohair (thin and handspun) if the fringe is to be tied to two sides only, or 100 g mohair if the fringe is to be tied to four sides.

METHOD
Thread the warp over 36 nails, using 100% cotton. Weave an edge of about 1 cm, using a double thickness of cotton.

When this has been completed, weave with the wool in the sequence given in **illustration 42(a)**. The vertical joins are shown in **illustration 14** and **photo 4.** Try to practice all the different techniques for joining.

As the various colours are woven separately, care should be taken to beat the web down evenly. The density of the weaving should be the same throughout.

Measure the width of the web now and then to make sure that it remains 35 cm throughout.

FINISHING
When the 1 cm cotton edge has been completed at the top, the length of the weaving should be checked before it is taken off the frame. Measure at the sides as well as in the middle of the weaving. It should be 65/66 cm throughout, if the edges are added. If the length is irregular, the web should be beaten down until the shape is completely rectangular.

The web can now be removed according to method (b) described in the chapter on finishing.

After the weaving has been removed and finished and the cotton edges folded back and sewn, the weaving is folded on the dotted line shown in **illustration 42(a)** with the right sides to the outside. Baste the sides together as shown in **illustration 42(b).**

FRINGE
Cut the mohair in lengths of 20 cm. Use three strands at a time and loop with a crochet hook through both layers of the cushion as shown in **illustration 42(c).** Tie each group of threads with an overhand knot.

Note: The fringe closes the sides of the cushion. If a fringe must be made on the other sides of the cushion as well, it is done as shown in **illustration 29(b).**

Photo 23
Cushions woven by members of the Kuil's River brance of the WAA and showing joining techniques

Illustration 42

(a) Pattern for a cushion

(b) The weaving is folded back before the fringe is made

(c) Making the fringe

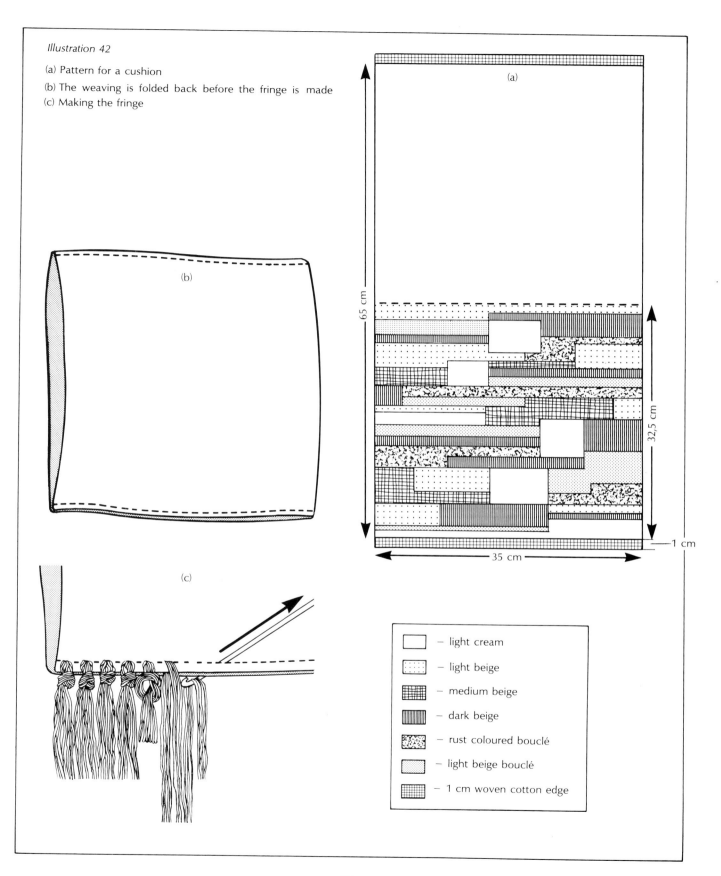

- light cream
- light beige
- medium beige
- dark beige
- rust coloured bouclé
- light beige bouclé
- 1 cm woven cotton edge

65 cm

32,5 cm

35 cm

1 cm

Tray-cloth and tea-cosy

TRAY-CLOTH AND TEA-COSY

Although the same techniques are used in this project as in project 2, weaving this tray-cloth and tea-cosy does pose some new challenges for the beginner. A new kind of weft thread, strips of fabric, is used, and for the tea-cosy one needs to learn how to weave a curve.

Later, when the weaver has gained experience, the technique of weaving with strips of fabric can be used to weave small rugs. As one usually has many small remnants of fabric, these items can be woven at little cost.

Cutting the strips takes some time, however. It is worth the trouble, as the texture obtained from these strips is quite different from that obtained when weaving with wool.

Choose colours to suit your own colour scheme.

SIZE
Tray-cloth:
28 × 40 cm
Tea-cosy:
28 × 24 cm

MATERIALS
Frame:
Frame 1
Warp:
100 g $\frac{8}{12}$ 100% cotton or any other strong 100% cotton
Weft:
1,5 m white 100% cotton material, 140 cm wide
Remnants in the following colours: Dark red, sea-green, dark grey, red and white check
25 g white cotton thread for the 1 cm edges
0,75 m dark red or white piping for the tea-cosy

PREPARING THE WEFT
Wash and iron the material.

Cut the cotton material into strips of 1 cm. The beginning and end should be cut at an angle. (See the strips of material in **photo 24**.) In this way the strips can be joined neatly where necessary. The tea-cosy is woven with strips cut on the bias to prevent them from fraying. The strips for the tray-cloth, on the other hand, are cut on the square, and they have a frayed effect when woven. When the article is finished off, the loose threads can be cut off.

The cotton edge is woven with one reel of string used for tying parcels. The string is first rolled into a skein, washed a few times to remove the glue and then bleached. The result is a soft white cotton thread.

Note: This cotton cannot be used as warp, only as weft. If you do not wish to go to so much trouble, you can weave the edge with white cotton crochet thread.

METHOD FOR WEAVING THE TRAY-CLOTH
Thread the warp with cotton thread over 29 nails. Weave an edge with the white cotton weft thread.

Weave with the strips of material, using the sequence given in **illustration 43(a)**. When the weft threads are inserted, the arcs should be quite high. Blocks of colour are linked vertically by means of dovetailing. Beat down the web evenly and remember to check the width of the web after every few rows.

FINISHING THE TRAY-CLOTH
When the 1 cm cotton edge has been completed at the top, the length of the weaving should be checked before it is removed from the frame.

Remove the web according to method (b) described in the chapter on finishing.

Note: The warp threads are sewn into the web, but the edge is not folded back.

Cut off loose threads and press with a steam iron if necessary.

METHOD FOR WEAVING
THE TEA-COSY
Illustration 43(b) shows the pattern of the cosy.

Note: Two panels have to be woven.

When the top curve has to be woven, this curve should first be drawn on to the warp threads. It may be necessary to undo the weaving and repeat the process a few times until the correct curve is achieved. **See photo 24.**

FINISHING THE TEA-COSY
As the weaving ends in a curve, it is not necessary to finish with a cotton edge. Remove the web according to method (b) described in the chapter on finishing.

Note: The open warp threads are sewn into the weaving. The cotton edge at the bottom is folded back and sewn to the back.

Photo 24
The curve of the tea-cosy is first drawn on to the warp and then woven

Place the piping between the two panels of the tea-cosy (right sides to the outside) so that it forms a neat ridge around the curve of the cosy. Baste carefully. The three layers can now be sewn either with a sewing-machine or by hand. Note that the tea-cosy is not turned inside out. The sewing is done on the outside.

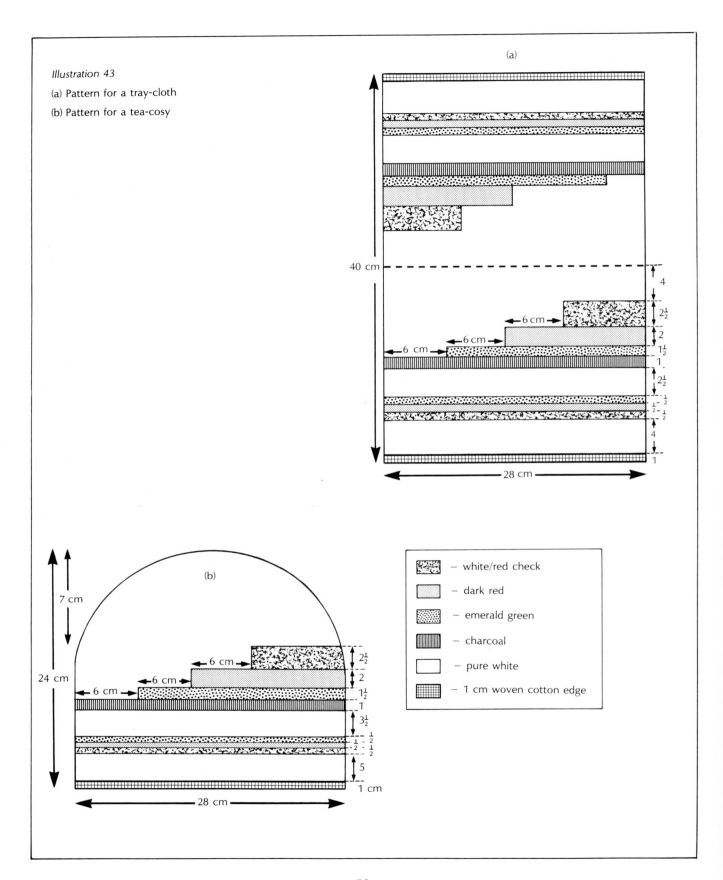

Illustration 43

(a) Pattern for a tray-cloth

(b) Pattern for a tea-cosy

Legend:
- white/red check
- dark red
- emerald green
- charcoal
- pure white
- 1 cm woven cotton edge

56

Photo 25
Tea-cosy and tray-cloth woven with fabric strips by Claudine Louw

Bib

BIB

The purpose of this project is to stimulate the weaver's creativity, and to show that frame weaving can be used for more than household articles and wall hangings. Handbags and even a pocket for a winter coat can be woven on a frame. For these articles you can use the colours, textures and designs of your choice.

This project also provides practice in dovetailing and a new method of tying the fringe. This method is, however, only for those who feel that they have mastered the basic weaving techniques.

Note: Only the weaving of a bib is described here. You can use it on clothes of your choice. The bib is fastened to the clothes with velcro, so that it can be removed for washing.

SIZE
20 × 30 cm (with tassels)

MATERIALS
Frame:
Frame 1
Warp:
25 g of 100% cotton crochet thread, grey or any colour that fits into the colour scheme
Weft:
Remnants of handspun wool in light, medium and dark grey, black, dark red, sea-green, dark sea-green bouclé or other textured thread

Note: The total weight of the wool is 75 g. The wool should not be thicker than double knit wool
20 cm velcro
20 cm × 15 cm grey iron-on vilene

METHOD
Thread the warp with cotton over 21 nails. Do not weave an edge.

Begin weaving the weft threads and weave according to the sequence given in **illustration 44(a)**. Use the dovetail technique if two colours are to be joined vertically.

Weft loops are left on the right side where necessary, according to the technique shown in **illustration 44(b)**.

From the middle of the panel you should choose your own combinations of colours and rectangles.

The length of the web should be 20 cm.

FINISHING
Do not weave an edge at the top of the weaving. Remove the web according to method (b) described in the chapter on finishing. Loose warp threads should be sewn neatly into the back of the weaving.

Weft threads on the right side of the web can be tied as shown in **illustration 44(c)**.

Sew one half of the velcro to the wrong side of the bib using hem stitch as shown in **illustration 44(a)**. Sew the other half to the clothing. Iron the vilene on to the back of the bib with a steam iron for a neat finish.

Illustration 44

(a) Pattern for a bib

(b) Loops on the edge of the weaving

(c) Weft loops are tied with some extra weft thread

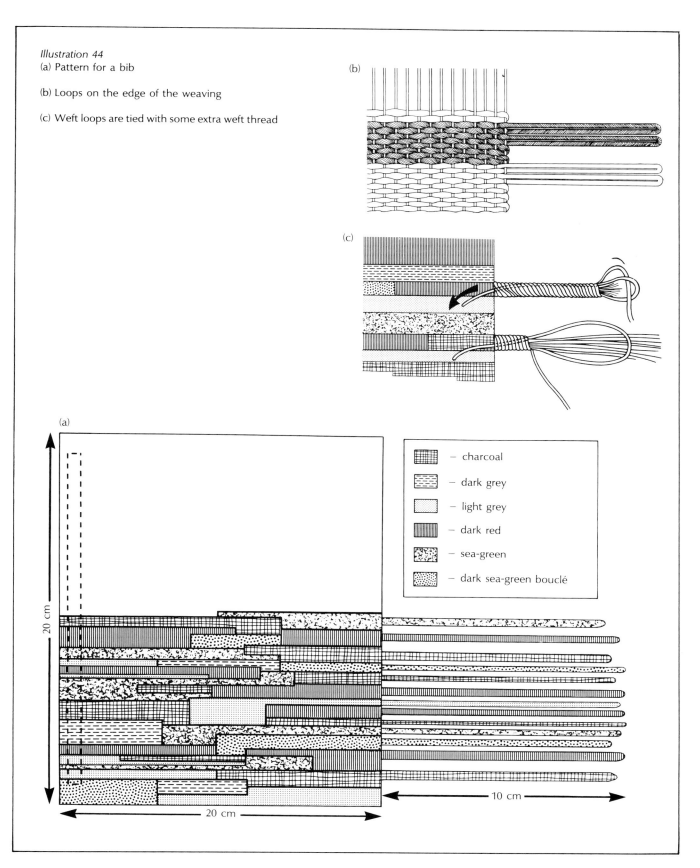

— charcoal

— dark grey

— light grey

— dark red

— sea-green

— dark sea-green bouclé

20 cm

20 cm

10 cm

Photo 26
Bib woven by Claudine Louw

Weed bag

WEED BAG

In this project neither horizontal lines nor vertical joins are used. The design uses curves and is quick and easy to weave. The beginner who has completed one or two of the previous projects will enjoy weaving this weed bag.

The techniques for weaving a curve and for making a Ghiordes knot are practised.

A carrier-bag can also be woven according to this method.

SIZE
32 cm × 32 cm without handles

MATERIALS
Frame:
Frame 1
Warp:
50 g unpolished flax
Weft:
  25 g wine red
100 g turquoise
  50 g charcoal   } handspun medium thick karakul
250 g light fawn
  50 g dark fawn
Handle:
1,5 m thick sisal

METHOD
Thread the warp over 33 nails, using flax. Weave an edge of 1 cm with a double thickness of flax.

The design shown in **illustration 45(a)** may be enlarged on a piece of cardboard. This will facilitate the weaving of the curves. Fasten the cardboard to the back of the frame with thumbnails. **See photo 5.**

Weave according to the diagram in **illustration 45(a)**, beginning with light fawn karakul.

When the length of the weaving is 32 cm, a few Ghiordes knots may be tied, according to method (a) on page 22. Cut lengths of 70 cm in charcoal and turquoise to do this.

The enlarged diagram may now be placed under the warp and the design drawn on the warp with a permanent marker. Weave the rest of the design in the numerical sequence shown in **illustration 45(a).**

Weave an edge of 1 cm with the flax at the top of the web.

FINISHING
Remove the web from the frame according to method (b) described in the chapter on finishing. Remember to fold the flaxen edge back and to hem-stitch it to the back of the weaving.

Fold the bag in two wrong sides together. Tie an overhand knot to one end of the rope and sew the end of the rope and two open sides of the bag together as shown in **illustration 45(b)**. The rope may have to be shortened. Sew the other end of the rope to the other sides as well.

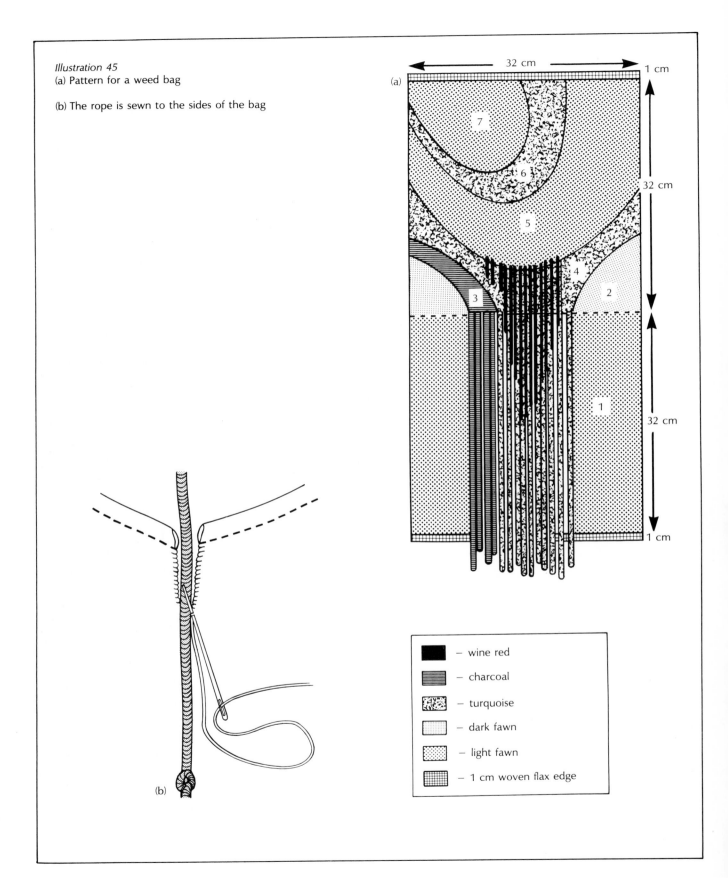

Illustration 45
(a) Pattern for a weed bag

(b) The rope is sewn to the sides of the bag

32 cm

1 cm

32 cm

32 cm

1 cm

(a)

(b)

■ – wine red

▤ – charcoal

▨ – turquoise

▧ – dark fawn

▧ – light fawn

▦ – 1 cm woven flax edge

Photo 27
Weed bag woven by Claudine Louw

Wall-hanging with curves

WALL-HANGING WITH CURVES

In this project the weaver can practise weaving curves, and techniques such as texture inlays, loop weaving, hatching, Soumak and Ghiordes knots. The curves are outlined with Soumak knots.

In this project the design is given and also the various techniques and knots. The weaver may use her own initiative and taste regarding the choice of colours. The hanging shown in **photo 28** was woven in shades of pink with dove grey as contrasting colour.

SIZE
Hanging after finishing but before framing: 50 × 50 cm

MATERIALS
Frame:
Frame 2
Warp:
75 g unpolished flax
Weft:
600 g handspun wool in main colour (preferably in different textures)
50 g mohair tops in main colour
50 g mohair tops in contrasting colour
50 g handspun wool in contrasting colour

METHOD
Thread the warp over 51 nails, using flax. Weave an edge of 1 cm with a double thickness of flax.

Illustration 46 gives the necessary information regarding techniques and knots.

Weave from the bottom up, and draw the curves on the warp as you go along. This weaving needs to be beaten down firmly; you are weaving a hanging and not a piece of cloth and therefore have to obtain a sturdy effect.

FINISHING
Weave an edge of 1 cm, remove the web from the frame, sew in the loose threads and sew the edges according to method (b) described in the chapter on finishing.

Note: No specifications for framing the hanging are given. Choose a method to suit your own taste.

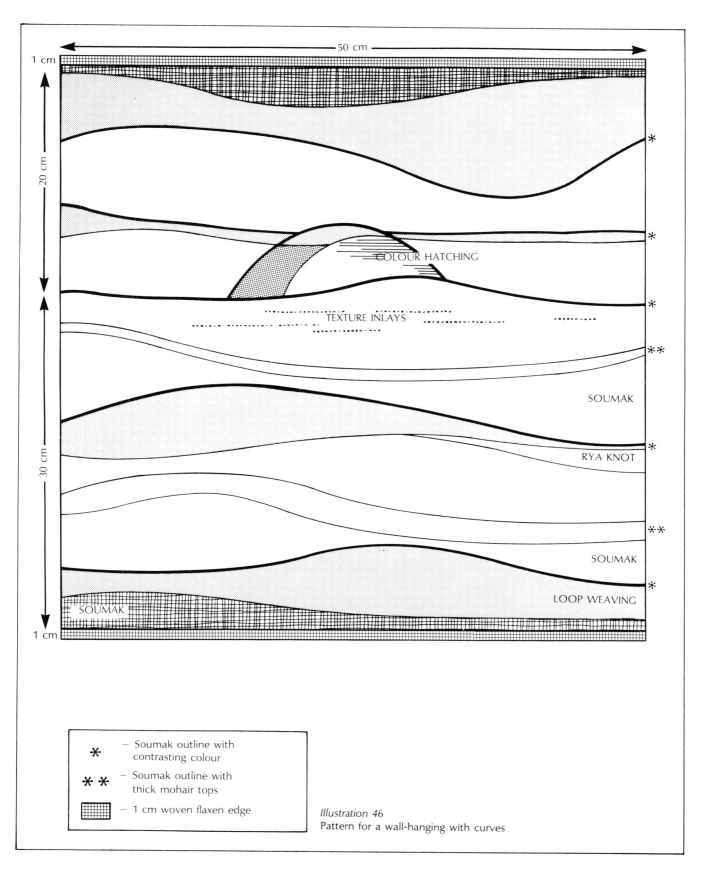

COLOUR HATCHING

TEXTURE INLAYS

SOUMAK

RYA KNOT

SOUMAK

LOOP WEAVING

SOUMAK

50 cm

1 cm

20 cm

30 cm

1 cm

*   – Soumak outline with contrasting colour

**   – Soumak outline with thick mohair tops

  – 1 cm woven flaxen edge

Illustration 46
Pattern for a wall-hanging with curves .

Photo 28
Wall-hanging with curves woven by Claudine Louw

Wall-hanging with landscape

WALL-HANGING WITH LANDSCAPE

This project is especially for those who prefer realism to abstract designs. Techniques such as textured inlays, curves, colour hatching, loop weaving and the looped Ghiordes knot are used here. A new technique, that of attaching pebbles, is also introduced. The design is given with specifications for the various techniques and knots, but not with instructions for the use of colours. this is again left to the weaver to decide.

By carefully examining the techniques and knots shown in **illustration 47(a)**, one will be able to adapt the design to suit one's personal taste. If the texture inlays at the top are increased, the sky will appear more overcast. More curves will give a more mountainous appearance to the landscape. The colours can be changed to suggest a sunset or a sunrise.

SIZE
After finishing but before framing:
    50 cm × 50 cm

MATERIALS
Frame:
Frame 2
Warp:
75 g unpolished flax
Weft:
150 g in various shades for the sky and texture inlays

100 g in various shades for hills
150 g in various shades for water
150 g for sand
150 g for texture in foreground (various textures)
In the hanging shown here, hessian was used for texture in the foreground
10-12 pebbles in shades that match the colour scheme

METHOD
Thread the warp over 51 nails, using flax. Weave an edge of 1 cm with a double thickness of flax.

Study **illustration 47(a)** and **photo 29** well before you begin to weave. The design can be drawn on the warp as you go along. For this project the weft threads need to be beaten down firmly.

Note: If pebbles are to be inserted, the background should first be woven. Place a pebble on top of the web. Use flax and a short darning needle and prepare a vertical warp over the pebble. Then weave through the warp and over the pebble. **See illustration 47(b).**

FINISHING
Weave an edge of 1 cm at the top, remove from the frame, sew in the loose threads and sew the edge according to method (b) described in the chapter on finishing.

Note: Specifications for framing the hanging are not given. This should be chosen to suit the weaver's own taste.

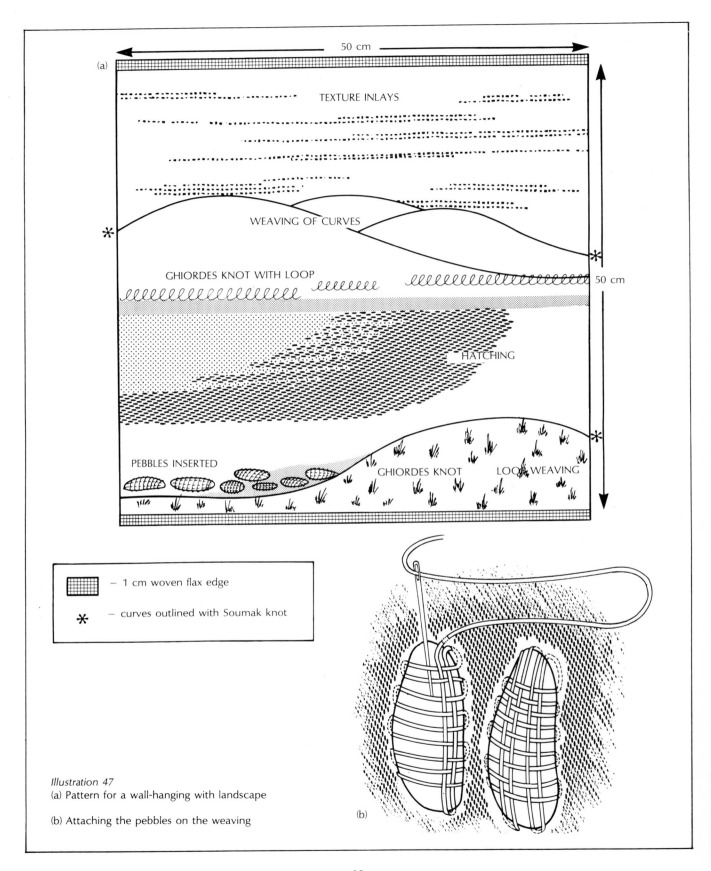

(a)

TEXTURE INLAYS

WEAVING OF CURVES

GHIORDES KNOT WITH LOOP

50 cm

HATCHING

PEBBLES INSERTED

GHIORDES KNOT   LOOP WEAVING

▦ – 1 cm woven flax edge

* – curves outlined with Soumak knot

(b)

Illustration 47

(a) Pattern for a wall-hanging with landscape

(b) Attaching the pebbles on the weaving

Photo 29
Wall-hanging by Claudine Louw

Two-panelled wall-hanging

TWO-PANELLED WALL-HANGING

This project illustrates a method of weaving large hangings on small frames. Frame 2 is used to weave two panels of the same size. When the first one is completed it is removed from the frame, the frame is warped again and the second panel is woven. The two panels are then placed next to each other. Loops at the top and a long fringe at the bottom enlarge the panels even more and provide a neat finish. The two panels are not attached to each other, but the design which overflows to the second panel brings unity to the whole. More than two panels can also be used.

Simple techniques are used in this hanging, which proves that the correct use of simple techniques can have extremely striking results. Here curves are woven and outlined with Soumak knots.

SIZE
120 cm × 50 cm (both panels before finishing)
120 cm × 90 cm (both panels with loops and fringe)

MATERIALS
Frame:
Frame 2
Warp:
2 × 75 g unpolished flax
Weft:
300 g medium thick dark grey to black
200 g medium thick dove-grey to light grey
150 g very thick texture in light grey
350 g medium thick light cream
200 g very thick texture in light cream
150 g medium thick wine red
150 g medium thick turquoise
 50 g very thick texture in turquoise
Finishing:
1 × 1,25 m rod (painted black)

METHOD
Thread the warp over 51 nails, using flax. Weave an edge of 1 cm with a double thickness of flax against the top and bottom row of nails. The design may be enlarged on a piece of cardboard and then drawn on the warp with a permanent marker.

Study the directions given in **illustration 48** and **photo 30** well before starting to weave.

Weave the first curve with dark grey/black wool. Outline this curve with Soumak knots in wine red wool. All the curves are woven in this way. The curves are outlined with Soumak knots in a contrasting colour so that a slight ridge is formed. **See photo 6.** Complete the first panel, remove from the frame and prepare the second warp. Complete the second panel and remove from the frame.

FINISHING
Both panels are finished according to method (a) described in the chapter on finishing. They are then turned length wise and placed next to each other.

The following loops, all 10 cm in length, are woven, each on a separate warp:

2 in dark grey/black wool, 6 cm in width
1 in dark grey/black wool, 4 cm in width
2 in wine red wool, 2 cm in width
1 in wine red wool, 5 cm in width
1 in dove-grey wool, 5 cm in width
2 in light grey wool, 8 cm in width
3 in turquoise wool, 1,5 cm in width

Note: When these loops are folded, they are of course 5 cm in length.

When they are completed, they are folded over and attached to the top of the panels. The rod is then inserted and the panels arranged so that they touch each other.

The fringe is tied to the bottom. The colours of the fringe should be the same as that of the weft threads immediately above. The length of the fringe varies between 20 and 40 cm. **Photo 30** shows how the length of the fringe is varied to suit the design.

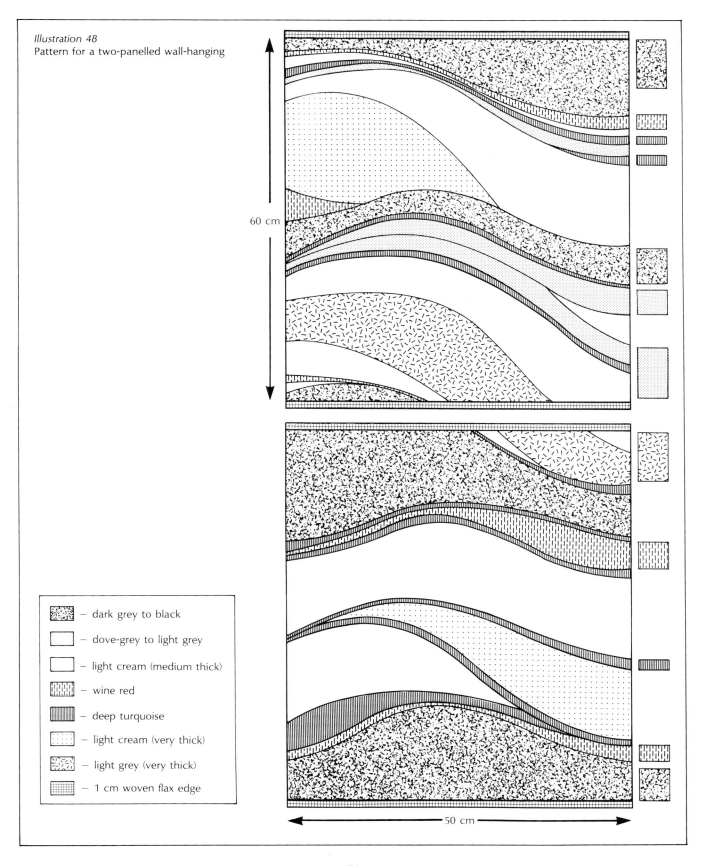

Illustration 48
Pattern for a two-panelled wall-hanging

60 cm

50 cm

– dark grey to black

– dove-grey to light grey

– light cream (medium thick)

– wine red

– deep turquoise

– light cream (very thick)

– light grey (very thick)

– 1 cm woven flax edge

Photo 30
Two-panelled wall-hanging by Claudine Louw

Wall-hanging with bamboo and reeds

WALL-HANGING WITH BAMBOO AND REEDS

The weaver who likes to work with many different textures will enjoy this project. Three separately woven strips are joined here and there with bits of bamboo and reeds. The hanging is mainly cream-coloured with shades of yellow and dove-grey as contrasts. Interesting textures such as strips of leather, hessian, unbleached calico and raffia are used.

The hanging is finished with bamboo rods through the top and bottom. This is a quick and easy way of finishing and fits in with the overall design.

SIZE
45 cm × 70 cm

MATERIALS
Frame:
Frame 1
Piece of cardboard 3 cm × 50 cm
Warp:
50 g unpolished flax
Weft:
200 g medium thick cotton (light cream)
150 g unevenly spun wool (light cream)
 50 g wool remnants in shades of yellow
 25 g wool remnants in dove-grey
Strips of unbleached calico (1 cm in width)
Strips of hessian, 2 cm in width
A few strings of natural raffia
Bamboo: 7 × 32-20 cm lengths (1 cm in diameter)
Reeds: 5 × 32 cm lengths
        21 × 14 cm lengths
Finishing:
2 bamboo rods 45 cm in length and 2 cm in diameter.

METHOD
Thread a warp around 19 nails with flax. Skip one nail and thread a second warp around 7 nails. Skip a nail and thread a third warp over 13 nails. There are therefore three warps, 18 cm, 6 cm and 12 cm in width and with spaces of 2 cm between them. Weave the cardboard through the warp threads just above the bottom nails. See **illustration 49(a)**. Weave an edge of 0,5 cm with a double thickness of flax as a base for each of the three strips.

Study the instructions given in **illustration 49(a)** and **photo 32** before weaving the wall-hanging.

Note: The central strip is woven in shades of yellow, and with raffia, strips of hessian and reeds. The strips on the sides are woven with cream-coloured wool and cotton, with a few rows of yellow wool, raffia, hessian or dove-grey wool as contrast. Use flax or raffia to insert the bamboo and reeds.

Begin weaving against the cardboard strip and continue until the first piece of bamboo has to be inserted. Place one of the 32 cm lengths over the central and right strips. Use flax or raffia and attach the bamboo to the weaving according to the method described in **illustration 49(b)** and **photo 31**. Continue weaving for a few rows on the central and right-hand strips, and then place a 32 cm length of reed on these strips just above the bamboo. Attach the reed in the same way as the bamboo.

When the weaving is about 4 cm from the top row of nails, an edge of 0,5 cm is woven at the top of each strip.

FINISHING
The piece of cardboard is removed from the weaving and bamboo rods inserted at the top and bottom between the warp threads. This method of finishing is described in detail in the chapter on finishing, and also shown in **illustrations 31 and 32**.

Photo 31
Technique for attaching bamboo and reeds to the weaving

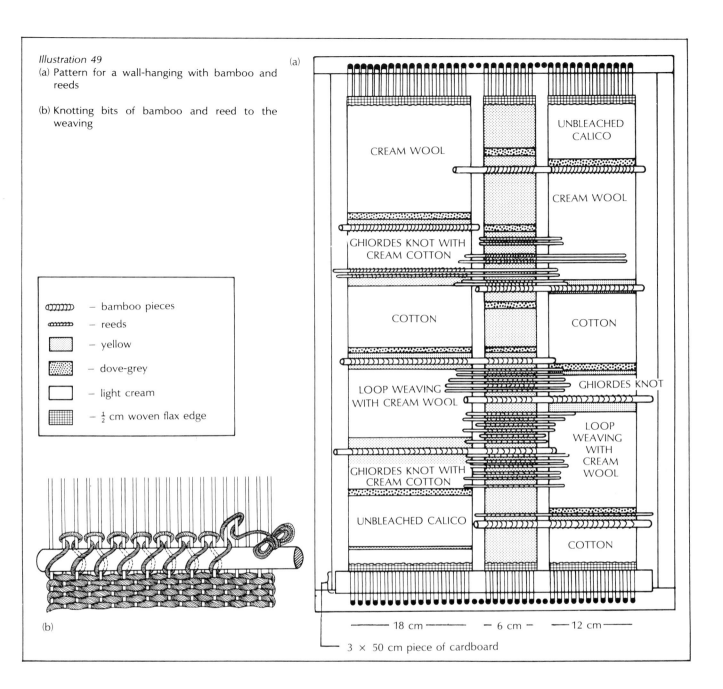

Illustration 49

(a) Pattern for a wall-hanging with bamboo and reeds

(b) Knotting bits of bamboo and reed to the weaving

(a)

Key:
- ⬭⬭⬭ – bamboo pieces
- ⬭⬭ – reeds
- ▨ – yellow
- ▦ – dove-grey
- ▢ – light cream
- ▦ – ½ cm woven flax edge

CREAM WOOL

UNBLEACHED CALICO

CREAM WOOL

GHIORDES KNOT WITH CREAM COTTON

COTTON

COTTON

LOOP WEAVING WITH CREAM WOOL

GHIORDES KNOT

LOOP WEAVING WITH CREAM WOOL

GHIORDES KNOT WITH CREAM COTTON

UNBLEACHED CALICO

COTTON

—— 18 cm —— – 6 cm – —— 12 cm ——

3 × 50 cm piece of cardboard

(b)

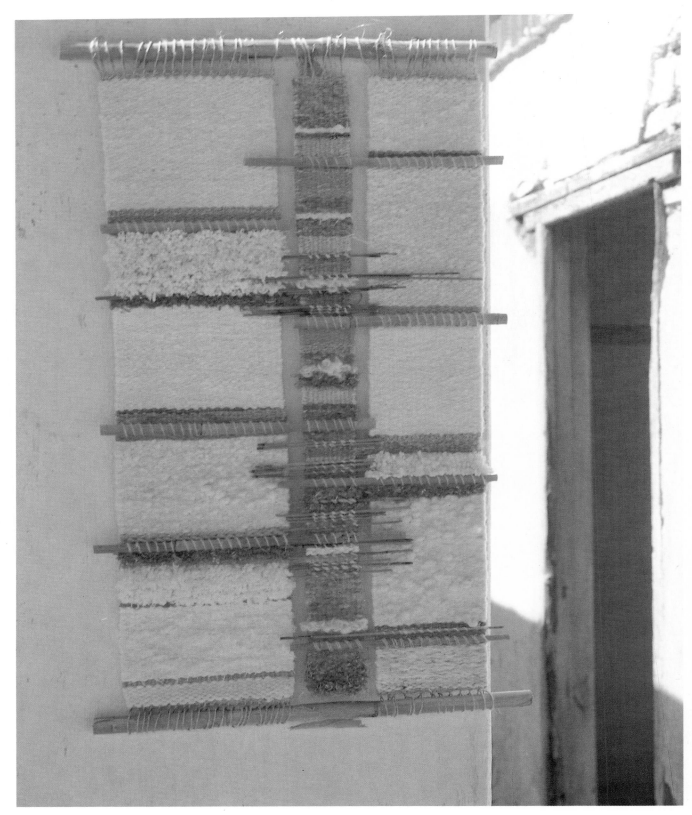

Photo 32
Wall-hanging with bamboo and reeds by Claudine Louw

Wall-hanging with buildings

WALL-HANGING WITH BUILDINGS

In this project a number of joining techniques and knots are used as part of the design. Soumak and Ghiordes knots give a three-dimensional effect to the roofs of the buildings.

The wall-hanging is woven in one basic colour. Variety is provided by the many different shades of the colour, and the different textures. Added contrast is provided by the gold thread.

You should have mastered the vertical slit and dove-tail techniques of joining before attempting this project, as they are an important part of the design. Project 2 provided practice in these techniques, and the cushion also matches this hanging. An interesting method of finishing, which enlarges the hanging considerably, is used. The method of attaching the weaving to hessian and stretching it over wood or pasteboard is described in the chapter on finishing.

SIZE
Weaving:
45 cm × 60 cm
Weaving on hessian background:
60 cm × 80 cm

MATERIALS
Frame:
Frame 2
Warp:
75 g unpolished flax

Weft:
300 g medium thick wool/cotton/mohair in medium to dark tones of cream (buildings and windows)
250 g thinner wool, cotton or mohair in light to medium tones of cream (sky)
 50 g light cream pearl cotton (sun)
 25 g gold crochet, knitting or embroidery thread
Finishing:
hessian, 80 cm × 100 cm
pasteboard, 60 cm × 80 cm
brown paper, 50 cm × 70 cm
cold glue

METHOD
Thread the warp over 46 nails, using flax. Weave an edge of 1 cm with a double thickness of flax.

The design may be enlarged on a piece of cardboard and drawn on to the warp with a permanent marker.

Study the instructions given in **illustration 50** and **photo 33** before you start weaving.

The darker tones are used in the roofs and windows. The flat roofs are outlined with gold thread. Medium tones are used for buildings and the various joining techniques are used between buildings. The pearl cotton is used for weaving the sun by means of slit-joining technique. **See photo 7.** The sky is woven in medium to light tones and finally an edge of 1 cm is woven when the length of the weaving is 60 cm.

FINISHING
The web is removed from the frame and finished according to method (a) described in the chapter on finishing. It can then be sewn on a piece of hessian and stretched over a board of pressed wood. The chapter on finishing describes these methods in detail.

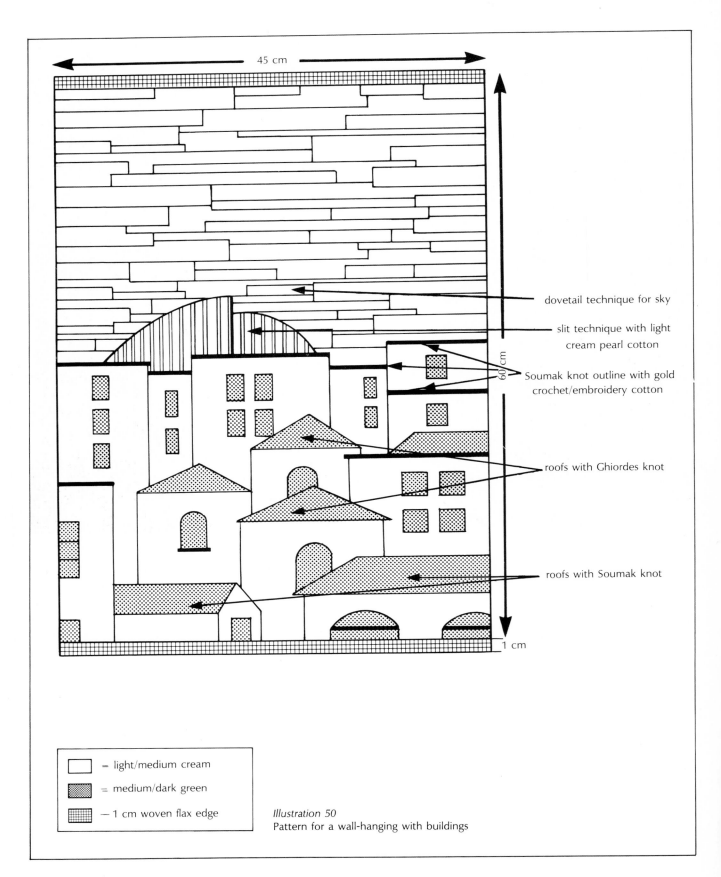

dovetail technique for sky

slit technique with light cream pearl cotton

Soumak knot outline with gold crochet/embroidery cotton

roofs with Ghiordes knot

roofs with Soumak knot

45 cm

60 cm

1 cm

☐ = light/medium cream

▦ = medium/dark green

▦ — 1 cm woven flax edge

Illustration 50
Pattern for a wall-hanging with buildings

Photo 33
Wall-hanging by Claudine Louw

Weavers guilds of South Africa

PRETORIA WEAVERS GUILD, 331 Boom Street, Pretoria, 0002.

SECUNDA WEAVERS AND SPINNERS, P.O. Box 197, Secunda, 2302.

ERMELO SPINNERS AND WEAVERS, P.O. Box 886, Ermelo, 2350.

POTCHEFSTROOM WEAVERS GUILD, 6 Louis Leipoldt Street, Potchefstroom, 2520.

NEWCASTLE WEAVERS GUILD, P.O. Box 9246, Newcastle, 2940

EMTSHEZI SPINNERS AND WEAVERS, P.O. Box 37, Winterton, 3340.

MIDLANDS SPINNERS AND WEAVERS, 14 Acutt Road, Hilton, 3245.

DURBAN HANDWEAVERS AND SPINNERS GUILD, 12 Dawn Crescent, Westville, 3630.

LOWER SOUTH COAST WEAVERS GUILD, P.O. Box 120, Margate, 4275.

EAST LONDON WEAVERS, 87 Hillcrest Drive, Beacon Bay, East London, 5241.

GRAHAMSTOWN WEAVERS AND SPINNERS GUILD, 21 Bedford Street, Grahamstown, 6140.

SOUTHERN CAPE WEAVERS GUILD, 234 Jan van Riebeeck Road, Oudtshoorn, 6620.

FRASERBURG STOKPERDJIEKLUB-WEWERSGILDE/HOBBIES CLUB-WEAVERS GUILD, P.O. Box 39, Fraserburg, 6960.

DIE KAAPSE WEWERSGILDE/CAPE WEAVERS GUILD, 4 De Villiers Road, Kenilworth, 7700.

STELLENBOSCH-WEWERSGILDE/STELLENBOSCH WEAVERS GUILD, P.O. Box 3031, Coetzenburg, 7602.

WEAVERS GUILD OF SOUTH WEST AFRICA/NAMIBIA, P.O. Box 3705, Windhoek, 9000.

WEWERSGILDE VAN OVS/WEAVERS GUILD OF OFS, P.O. Box 11188, Universitas, Bloemfontein, 9322.

JOHANNESBURG WEAVERS GUILD, P.O. Box 52570, Saxonwold, 2132

DIE NOORDWES-KAAP WEWERSGILDE/NORTHERN CAPE WEAVERS GUILD, Private Bag X101, Calvinia, 8190.

Bibliography

Beitler, E. J. & Lockhart, B. C. *Design for you,* John Wiley and Sons Inc., New York, 1969

Brostoff, L. *Weaving a tapestry,* Interweave Press Inc., 1982.

Collingwood, P. *The techniques of rug weaving,* Faber and Faber Ltd., London, 1968.

Dendel, E. W. *Needleweaving,* Thomas Nelson & Sons Ltd., London, 1971.

Droop, J. *Rugmaking,* G. Bell & Sons Ltd., London, 1971.

Fletcher, J. *Simply weaving,* Wilson & Horton Ltd., Auckland, 1980.

Handwoven Interweave Press Inc., Vol. IX No. 2, March/April 1988.

Handwoven Interweave Press Inc, Vol. IX, No. 5, November/December 1988.

Holland, N. *The weaving primer,* Chilton Book Company, 1978.

Holland, S. K. *All about creative textiles,* Oxford University Press, 1987.

Huxel, A. S. *Kreatives Bilderweben,* Falken-Verlag, 1986/1988.

Joicey, H. B. *An eye on the environment,* London, Bill & Hyman, 1986.

Kurtz, C. S. *Designing for weaving,* Hastings House Publ., 1981.

Liebler, B. *Hands on weaving,* Interweave Press Inc., 1986.

Pearson, A. *Tapestry weaving,* B.T. Batsford Ltd., London, 1984.

Raubenheimer, M. *En die mens weef,* Heer Drukkers, Pretoria.

Regensteiner, E. *The art of weaving,* Studio Vista Ltd., London, 1970.

Thomson, F. P. *Tapestry: Mirror of history,* David & Charles (Publishers) Ltd., London, 1980.

Tovey, J. *The technique of weaving,* B.T. Batsford Ltd., London, 1983.

Van der Merwe, M. & Basson, R. *Die tuiswewer,* Tafelberg-Uitgewers Bpk., Kaapstad, 1984.

Waldrop, D. *Easy to weave wall decorations,* Craft Course Publishers, 1977.

Wilson, J. *Soumak workbook,* Interweave Press Inc., 1982.

Znamierowski, N. *Weaving,* Evans Brothers, London, 1973.